JANET DeCLAY
FORT APACHE INDIAN
RESERVATION, ARIZONA

EARL FLETCHER
LANESBOROUGH, MASSACHUSETTS

PAT O'BRACK
HILLSBORO, NEW MEXICO

JOHN CHRISTENBERRY
HALE COUNTY, ALABAMA

JUDIE TALLICHET
SPRINGHILL SCHOOL
BELGRADE, MONTANA

CAROLYN JOYCE KING, KATHERINE ANN COLE,
SYBIL ANDERSEN BLEDSOE (FROM LEFT).
NEBO PLANTATION, MISSISSIPPI

LISA TODD'S SCULPTURE
SPRINGHILL SCHOOL
BELGRADE, MONTANA

JAMES "SON" THOMAS
LELAND, MISSISSIPPI

KRISTIN CHERONIS
GRASSHOPPER, ARIZONA

Back Roads
AMERICA
A Portfolio of Her People

By Thomas O'Neill
Photographed by Ira Block

Prepared by the Special Publications Division
National Geographic Society, Washington, D.C.

BACK ROADS AMERICA

By THOMAS O'NEILL
Photographed by IRA BLOCK

Published by
    The National Geographic Society
    GILBERT M. GROSVENOR, *President*
    MELVIN M. PAYNE, *Chairman of the Board*
    OWEN R. ANDERSON, *Executive Vice President*
    ROBERT L. BREEDEN, *Vice President,*
       Publications and Educational Media

Prepared by
    The Special Publications Division
    DONALD J. CRUMP, *Editor*
    PHILIP B. SILCOTT, *Associate Editor*
    RON FISHER, *Managing Editor*
    MARY ANN HARRELL, *Consulting Editor*
    CHARLES E. HERRON, *Picture Editor*
    SUEZ B. KEHL, *Art Director*
    TONI EUGENE, KATHLEEN F. TETER, *Senior*
      Researchers; BROOKE J. KANE, *Researcher;*
      AMY GOODWIN, DONNA B. KERFOOT,
      Assistant Researchers

Illustrations and Design
    JODY BOLT, *Consulting Art Director*
    CYNTHIA BREEDEN, TURNER HOUSTON,
      MARIANNE R. KOSZORUS, *Designers;*
      HOLLY BOWEN, KENNETH R. SHRADER,
      Design Assistants
    JOHN D. GARST, JR.; PETER J. BALCH,
      MARGARET DEANE GRAY, PATRICIA J. KING,
      SUSAN SANFORD, *Map Research, Design,*
      and Production
    JANE H. BUXTON, CHRISTINE ECKSTROM LEE,
      JANE R. MCCAULEY, TOM MELHAM,
      H. ROBERT MORRISON, *Picture Legends*

Engraving, Printing, and Product Manufacture
    ROBERT W. MESSER, *Manager*
    GEORGE V. WHITE, *Production Manager*
    JUNE L. GRAHAM, *Production Project Manager*
    MARK R. DUNLEVY, RICHARD A. MCCLURE,
      RAJA D. MURSHED, CHRISTINE A. ROBERTS,
      DAVID V. SHOWERS, GREGORY STORER,
      Assistant Production Managers
    SUSAN M. OEHLER, *Production Staff Assistant*
    DEBRA A. ANTONINI, PAMELA A. BLACK,
      BARBARA BRICKS, JANE H. BUXTON, MARY
      ELIZABETH DAVIS, ROSAMUND GARNER,
      NANCY J. HARVEY, JANE M. HOLLOWAY,
      SUZANNE J. JACOBSON, ARTEMIS S.
      LAMPATHAKIS, JONATHAN A. LAZZARINI,
      AMY E. METCALFE, CLEO PETROFF, MARCIA
      ROBINSON, KATHERYN M. SLOCUM,
      MARGARET J. TINSLEY, *Staff Assistants*
    BRIT AABAKKEN PETERSON, *Index*

Preceding pages: Narrow and winding, a dirt road in Wyoming's Wind River Range suggests the lure of America's byways. Along such back roads, travelers may find adventure, beauty, vanishing folkways—or a fresh-produce stand. Mrs. A. C. Cruse (page 1) sells fruits and vegetables by the side of State 60 in northern Georgia. Hardcover design: A country road wanders through the hills of Virginia.

*A*mish buggies anchor a volleyball net at the Middle Creek Wildlife Management Area in Pennsylvania. Families from the region's large farming community frequently gather at the refuge to picnic, hike, fish—and bird-watch. The 5,000-acre preserve attracts waterfowl—largely ducks, swans, and geese—migrating along the Atlantic flyway.

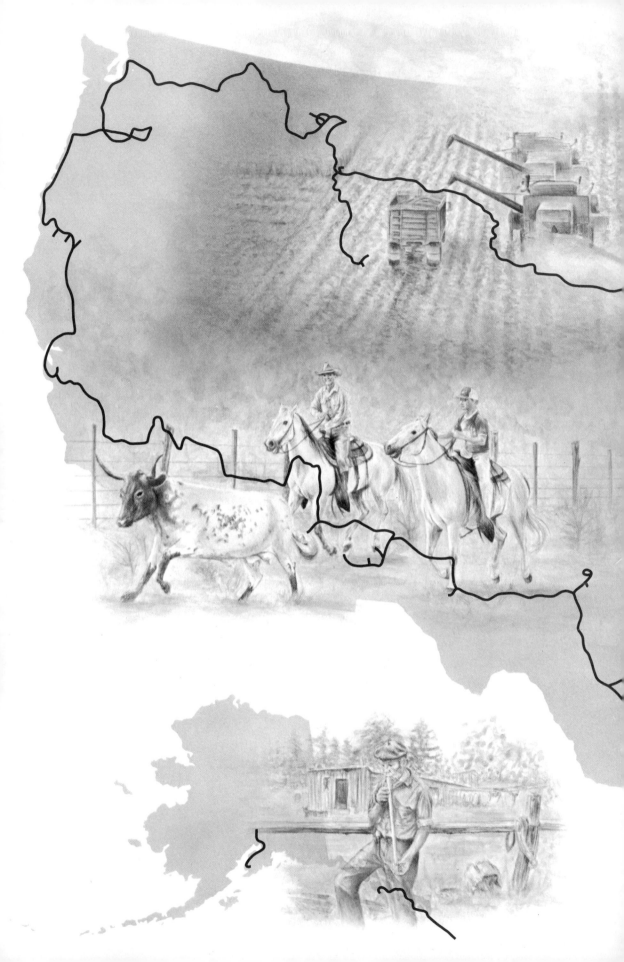

Prologue
Page 8

WINTER
Page 11

SPRING
Page 54

SUMMER
Page 97

AUTUMN
Page 152

Index and
Acknowledgments
Page 196

Back Roads
AMERICA

——————— Tom and Ira's Route

Prologue

TRAVELING ACROSS THE COUNTRY is an American dream. To climb aboard a bus or a train, or hop onto a motorcycle, or slip into a car and go—just *go*—is a basic romantic impulse. Movement is freedom, and to travel the breadth of the country is to proclaim that freedom in a bold and ebullient way.

The geography of the United States is now well mapped, and the regional cultures well chronicled. Yet the variety of people and places is so rich that a cross-country traveler is bound to discover something new. As the miles pass, the sense of exploration—somewhat atrophied in our modern day—gradually reasserts itself.

The dream can take shape at any stage of life. Mine began on a Sunday in central Illinois when I was a crew-cut boy. My parents had gathered the children together for a drive south to a town named Paris. Mother had heard that the flat farmland began to roll and rise in hills near there. After two hours of driving we reached our destination, and all around us was cropland, flat as a tabletop. Thinking we hadn't gone far enough, we continued down the road, but another hour of driving didn't produce one hill or swell of earth.

During that day my midwestern imagination had not been content with gently rolling countryside; it had become landscaped with mighty bluffs, plateaus, and mountains. When my parents finally turned the car toward home, my mind continued to travel, passing rivers and towns whose names I had read on maps, until I reached mountains that rose like thrones. I pictured myself being invited into a smoke-scented cabin for a meal of venison and berry pie. How unfair of my parents to have stopped south of Paris, Illinois. The rest of the country, I believed, was just down that road.

I found the road again, for it can appear anywhere and be designated by any number; you need only realize that it can carry you across the country. This time it stretched north from Washington, D.C. It was February 1979; a blizzard blew. Assigned to write a book about traveling through America, I had the opportunity at last to follow the road.

In nine months I covered 20,000 miles in a van outfitted and stocked for roaming. I had no plotted route, no sheaf of reservations, no address book of contacts. My editors in Washington had simply instructed me to stay away from cities and interstate highways.

So I wandered the back roads, stitching my route from small town to small town, most of them with a population of fewer than 3,000 people. Photographer Ira Block followed in a van of his own some two to four weeks behind, catching up occasionally for certain events. We were looking for people and for activities—a longhorn cattle rancher in Texas, an ice harvest in Vermont — that were emblematic of their geographical regions; that owed their vitality to the open land and to the close-knit community feelings that back roads life can offer.

In 1926 Will Rogers said: "Americans are getting like a Ford car—they all have the same parts, the same upholstering and make exactly the same noises."

Now, half a century later, the homogenization of America has intensified, leaving Main Street and the man on the street looking and sounding much the same across the country. Nevertheless, following country roads into small towns offered me the chance to find ways of life that have thus far escaped the pall of uniformity.

Superhighways are convenient and often necessary. There even can be a cathartic aspect to rushing along an interstate. Yet, in the end, a multilane trip produces tunnel vision. Speed is mandatory, so the traveler allows himself few peripheral glances, and the thought of the destination eclipses the process of getting there. If the high-speed driver has the opportunity to talk, other than to his radio, it is primarily with people who service the interstates: gas station attendants, waitresses, motel clerks.

If time can be indulged and speed forgotten, there is no more instructive or pleasurable way of seeing the country than by traveling on the back roads. You're encouraged to stop and talk with a variety of people, if only to keep from getting lost. The landscape is brought closer. You can see how fast the water in a creek is flowing, which wild flowers are blooming, how high the firewood is stacked, how deep the manure is spread. You can see the faces of the people you pass, read the signs on buildings, and, best of all, stop the car in the middle of nowhere and stretch and smell and believe for an instant that you could travel for the rest of your days.

One spring afternoon in Alabama I pulled into a service station in a six-block-long town. The attendant idly jammed the gas nozzle into the tank of my van and, seeing my District of Columbia license plates, just as idly asked, "Where're you going?"

"I don't know," I answered.

"You lost?" he asked, somewhat puzzled.

"No, I'm traveling across the country. No particular place to go. Probably reach California, and maybe Alaska, in the summer."

"California and Alaska," he slowly repeated as he wiped his hands with a rag. "I hear it's nice out there."

He fell silent. Soon the tank filled up, and I paid the money. Still the attendant said nothing. I started the engine and had begun to pull out when he turned from the pump and, with a trace of a smile, asked, "Need a partner?"

Down the road, I looked into the rearview mirror and saw the attendant gazing after me as he continued wiping his hands. I believe he imagined California and Alaska at the end of that narrow, pasture-lined road. I believe he had an American dream.

JOHN J. GAPS III

The long and the short of it: Out to see America, a National Geographic team visits a county fair sideshow in Iowa. In nine months, photographer Ira Block and writer Tom O'Neill drove 20,000 miles of back roads to produce this book.

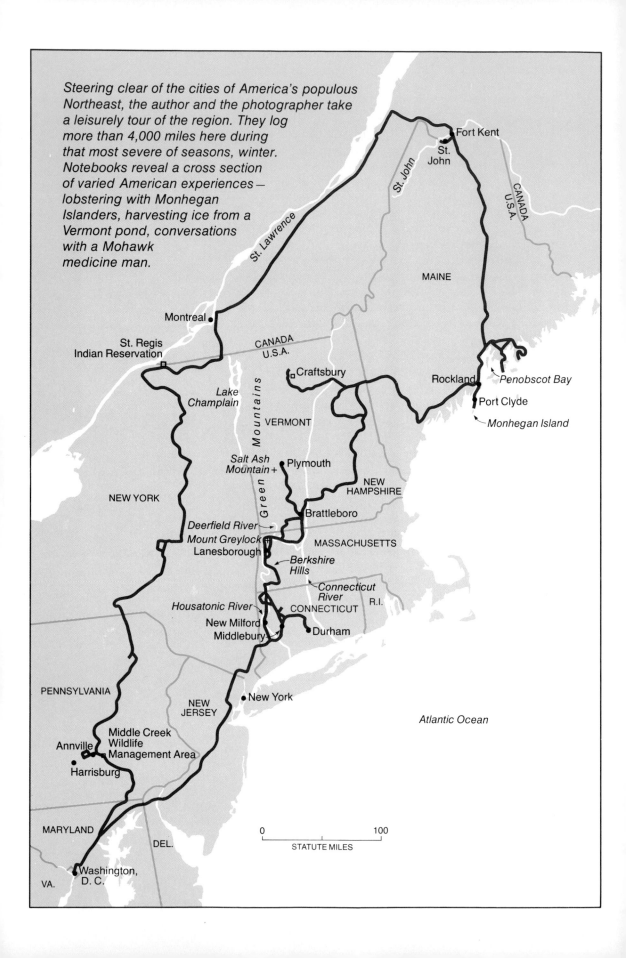

Steering clear of the cities of America's populous Northeast, the author and the photographer take a leisurely tour of the region. They log more than 4,000 miles here during that most severe of seasons, winter. Notebooks reveal a cross section of varied American experiences — lobstering with Monhegan Islanders, harvesting ice from a Vermont pond, conversations with a Mohawk medicine man.

Fort Kent

St. John

St. John

CANADA
U.S.A.

MAINE

St. Lawrence

Montreal

St. Regis
Indian Reservation

CANADA
U.S.A.

Craftsbury

Rockland

Penobscot Bay

Lake
Champlain

Port Clyde

Monhegan Island

VERMONT

Salt Ash
Mountain +

Plymouth

NEW
HAMPSHIRE

NEW YORK

Green Mountains

Brattleboro

Deerfield River
Mount Greylock +
Lanesborough

MASSACHUSETTS

Berkshire
Hills

Connecticut
River

R.I.

Housatonic River

CONNECTICUT

New Milford
Middlebury

Durham

New York

Atlantic Ocean

PENNSYLVANIA

NEW
JERSEY

Middle Creek
Wildlife
Management Area

Annville

Harrisburg

0   100

STATUTE MILES

MARYLAND

DEL.

Washington,
D. C.

VA.

Winter

MOST NEW ENGLANDERS have a story or two to tell about snow. It can be dramatic: roof-high drifts laying siege to a family for a week. Or romantic: lovers skiing across an unmarked field at moonrise. The entrepreneurial might tell of a lad making ninety dollars in one day shoveling sidewalks. Sometimes the story will even be slightly magical, almost fanciful, like the one I heard in Connecticut about a man who goes for sleigh rides in his backyard. At first I didn't believe it.

Two days before, on February 7, I had left Washington, D.C., to spend nine months driving around the country— back roads preferred. After two days on the road I wasn't certain whether I had yet slipped free of the orbits of large cities. I had pulled into New Milford, Connecticut, about 75 miles north of New York City—a sufficient distance, I thought—and was admiring the village green and a quaint hardware store when a local newspaperman told me, "Sorry. New Milford is exurbia." I drove farther in western Connecticut. Finding someone who rides a sleigh in his backyard surely would mean that I had reached the country.

So the next day I called on Carroll Mathews. He lives on the outskirts of Middlebury, in an area called Breakneck Hill. On this hill in 1781, Comte de Rochambeau, a French army officer who commanded troops during the American Revolution, camped while on his way to battle the British at Yorktown. According to colorful but questionable local tradition, an ox pulling a supply wagon slipped and broke its neck here. I sensed a slip in my own plans when I saw the Mathews house. It was a green ranch-style building, at home in either suburbia or exurbia, set in a neighborhood of similar houses. I saw no stable, no country lane. Convinced I had come to the wrong place, I knocked on the door and found myself facing a tall, silver-haired man wearing red suspenders. "You're just in time to go sleighing," he said.

The Mathews house is not an ordinary one, I found. Attached to the garage is a stable. Inside, three Morgan horses peered out of their stalls, and Carroll's two daughters, a son-in-law, and a grandson were bustling about, currying the horses, pulling harnesses off a wall. In the corner were two sleighs. Out back stretched a large yard fringed with woods. I believed. "I come from Maine," said Carroll, as he began to harness Daphne, a handsome nine-year-old mare. "I was born on a farm where my father used a horse to transport grain and deliver milk to town. I was brought up that way. When I first married, I bought horses of my own. I keep them now as a hobby."

"Sleighing is the only safe way to use horses in the winter," said his daughter, Nancy Pavan, who was combing a high-spirited bay mare named Donna. "If you want to have fun with horses all year round, you buy a sleigh," she said.

Carroll, 66, a retired school principal, had found his sleigh eight years before. "I was up in Berwick, Maine, in a barn with a man who was

New England One-horse open sleigh dashes through a Vermont field; Carroll
Mathews of Connecticut keeps a tight rein on a high-stepping Morgan. He and a few other

New Englanders make the best of their often raw winters by holding sleigh rallies at which they dress up in top hats and frock coats perfectly suited to the Currier & Ives settings.

trying to sell me a buggy. I didn't really want it, but while I was
dickering with this horse jockey I spotted a sleigh overhead. That was
what I wanted. While the fellow was in the house checking something, I
looked closely at it. When he came back I said, 'I'll give you a hundred
dollars cash in hand for the buggy if you'll throw in that sleigh.' Well,
that buggy is still in my basement, never been used."

Carroll restored the sleigh, and with its rich, fir-green color, black
leather seat, and elegant ash runners, it appeared to be in museum
condition, almost as good as in 1890 when it was built. Barn-scavenging
a year later, Sally and Bill Asevica—Carroll's other daughter and her
husband—spotted a sleigh they liked. This one was red, smaller, and
had more stylish lines. Bill said it was a "lady's sleigh," used primarily to
take the female faithful to and from church on Sundays.

When Daphne and Donna had been harnessed, we went outside
and for the rest of the afternoon went a-sleighing. We didn't go any-

Berkshire Hills

"I know more about my cows' pedigrees than my own," says Massachusetts dairy farmer Earl Fletcher. Earl feeds his 110 registered Jerseys five times each day and milks sixty of them every morning and evening. Leading an easier life, Thomas Q. Pussycat (below) pauses during barn patrol to accept the friendly lick of a rough bovine tongue.

where except in a circle inside the yard, and the scenery was only a line of trees and the backs of a few houses. But something about the crunch of snow under the runners, the whip of air on our cheeks, the jangling of bells on the harnesses, and the sight of manes flying brought a flush of excitement. Carroll stood near the stable most of the time, pleased to watch his family at play. But when Donna began to toss her head and strain at the reins, he climbed swiftly into the red sleigh, softly commanded, "Walk," and the frisky mare stepped with dignity around the yard, as if she were taking her riders to church.

The next day, under a brilliant sky, I met the Mathews family at a farm outside Durham. In a field next to the road some forty sleighs glided in a circle. The occasion was a sleigh rally, the winter version in New England of a horse show. Sleigh rallies were first held in Connecticut, according to participants. Eighteen years before, the story goes, a man named Henry R. Hoppe from Hartford County invited some friends who owned sleighs to join him in a field to take a few turns. Before long, some passersby stopped to watch. The pastime caught on, and a new event was born.

No doubt Mr. Hoppe would have stayed at home on this particular Sunday. The weather was more suitable for a dogsled race. Brutal cold had hit the area overnight, and the temperature was staying below zero. But the season's first heavy snow had fallen only a few days earlier, and apparently nothing would deter the sleighers from the year's inaugural rally. Displaying his Maine hardiness, Carroll worked without gloves, rigging the harnesses and taping the horses' ankles.

The Currier & Ives event produced the most entertainment. Sleighers attempted to look as if they had stepped out of one of the popular 19th-century winter scenes lithographed by Nathaniel Currier and James Merritt Ives. Out came the men dressed in frock coats and top hats, the women in fur hats and muffs, with robes laid across their laps. With their costumed riders and prancing horses, the sleighs circled the field, resembling a procession on an antique clock tower.

The awards are numerous, so everyone wins something. By day's end the Mathews family had won two ribbons, both orange. "I've seen a lot of ribbons in my time, but never an orange one," Nancy said with a laugh. Carroll and I had competed in the "gentleman's class," but with our red faces we didn't look much like gentlemen. No, we looked like what we were—two cold joyriders enjoying a day in the country.

In a book of Currier & Ives prints you can flip from a winter scene to one of a paddleboat riffling a river on a mild spring night. In New England no such alternative existed for me. The next day, in polar cold, I drove north into Massachusetts. I followed the frozen Housatonic River for several miles and then branched off through ice-encrusted hills, part of the narrow belt of uplands that stretches from western Connecticut to the Green Mountains in Vermont.

In the Berkshire Hills of Massachusetts, a crowded resort area in summer, the cold appeared to have emptied the roads and sidewalks as effectively as an air raid would have. A feeling of dormancy hung over the rural landscape with its empty white fields and boarded-up cabins. If I wanted to see anyone in this dairy farm country, I realized, I would have to visit a barn.

When I arrived at Jersey Acres Farm in Lanesborough at 5 a.m., in thick darkness, Earl Fletcher, 56, was already dishing out grain to his herd. A few heads turned, revealing the sweet, dumb faces of the Jersey breed. The low-ceilinged barn was peculiarly odorless, as if the early morning cold had frozen all smell. Across the barn Earl's sister, Rhetta, 59, who operates the farm with Earl, was feeding the calves. A couple of tomcats, one with a chewed ear, huddled in the straw.

The day before, Earl had invited me to spend a day at work with him. As I watched him move down a row of cows with his grain bucket, he turned and said, "We have to do the milking twice a day, 365 days a year." Unlike some crop farmers, who can take sunny vacations in winter while the fields lie fallow, a dairy farmer must face the question: "Who would milk the cows?"

"We're not our own bosses," Earl said with a chuckle. "The cows are." Yet if the job is a tyrant, Earl seems a dutiful subject. No one, especially his wife, Faith, a first-grade teacher, can say he's not devoted to his work. "Not even a marriage could disrupt his schedule," Faith told me. "On the morning of our wedding he delivered milk to town, plowed the driveway, and was late for the ceremony." Faith and Earl were married on a Saturday, and on Monday afternoon Earl was back milking cows. The honeymoon consisted of a weekend trip to Maine to visit some dairy farms.

When the feeding was finished, Earl picked up a hoe and began scraping manure into a gutter, where conveyor paddles moved it to a spreader outside. "Oh, I could probably make more money elsewhere," he said, peering at me from under a red cap. "But I don't know if it would be better. Only thing I know is that it's hard work. I get up at five, and when eight hours are up, it's just one o'clock. That's a darn short day. We still have six hours to go."

After the stalls were cleaned, Earl hauled the spreader across the road with a tractor and "decorated a field"—spread the manure over a cornfield. His 258-acre farm lies in a scenic valley. To the north is Mount Greylock, at 3,491 feet the highest point in the state. There once were five farms on the road where the Fletchers live, but now Jersey Acres, bought by Earl and Rhetta's father in 1930, is one of the last two. When the Fletchers retire, the farm will likely pass out of the family. Earl has two teenage daughters, both of whom can milk cows and drive a tractor, but, according to Earl, "they've found other interests."

At 6:30 the milking began. Earl's hired hand had arrived a few minutes earlier. Working two cows at a time, each man would bend and attach a metal four-cupped milking machine to a cow's udder. The machine's constant pulsation, like the opening and closing of a hand, drew milk from the udder into a tube that ran along the ceiling and into a stainless steel cooler. The Jersey, a small, usually fawn-colored cow developed on Jersey, an island in the English Channel, is famous for its rich, creamy milk. It is a minority breed, however, comprising about 10 percent of the dairy cows in the United States. Most farmers in the Berkshires raise Holsteins because of their greater milk and beef production. With sixty milkers, Earl's operation is about average in size. Large farms carry more than a hundred milkers. Exhibiting his strain of Yankee caution and thrift, Earl dismissed the notion of expansion. "It would be a case of buying more land, growing more feed. It's a never-ending cycle. I don't want to go into debt like the other fellow. Some farmers put in $2,000 per new cow. I don't like living like that."

Earl sounded a bit curmudgeonish about progress in general when Jim Alicata, of the United Cooperative Farmers, a local co-op, stopped by late in the morning to discuss analyzing Earl's feed to determine its nutritional value.

"This technology drives me buggy," Earl said. "Used to be you fed what you had and went along that way."

"Lot simpler, eh?" Jim responded.

"Yes, a lot simpler, and I think just as good."

"But," said Jim, "you didn't get as much milk."

"That's true," Earl said, "but that's about the only difference." With this grudging admission, Earl returned to his milking.

Outside the barn, Jim was diplomatic about the situation. "Earl's a typical New England farmer. He believes in letting the bugs get worked out before using a new system."

When the milking was completed and the cows were lying down, Earl guided me through the barn, crowded with hay bales and farm machinery. He pointed out the corn chopper and the hay baler he had

Green Mountains

Wintry crop harvested from a Vermont pond in February helps a back-to-nature summer camp keep its cool through July and August. Members of the Farm and Wilderness Foundation in Plymouth arrive (right) to cut the pond's frozen cap into blocks (below). Often a cube's removal requires five people—two to lift it, one to steady it, and two more to keep the first pair from slipping into the water (opposite). Dragged to an ice house and packed in sawdust, the ice will keep through the warm months ahead.

Letter-box labels reflect a rural pace at Packer's Corner Farm, a commune near Brattleboro, Vermont. City-weary artists founded the farm in 1968, hoping to create an inspirational atmosphere for their lives and work.

recently purchased, and he patiently explained the different additions to the barn. As Earl spoke of the improvements to Jersey Acres, I realized that beneath his suspicion of change, there existed, somewhat uneasily, a gradual acceptance of innovation. When I remarked that for a die-hard nonexpansionist he had enlarged his operation to some extent, Earl stopped, looked around, and sheepishly conceded, "Yes, Dad probably wouldn't recognize the place."

At 2:45, the afternoon routine began: feeding, cleaning, milking. Conversation drifted like smoke among the stalls, the topics ranging from Earl's happy subjects (the Boston Red Sox, horse racing) to sour ones (Washington bureaucrats, a farmers' strike). "I'd be a liar if I said this job wasn't monotonous at times," Earl said. "But you live for things that break up the monotony, to give you incentive. Like selling six heifers to India as part of a group of 300 that New England sent. Or watching those calves growing up, wondering how they'll do."

Late in the afternoon I walked up through a field behind the farm and looked down at the buildings—the red, irregularly shaped barn, the 200-year-old brick house. They anchored the landscape, implying a sense of permanence. The Fletchers, too, gave off a sense of stability, with their capacity for hard work and the acceptance of their lot. The daily routine sustained and ennobled this farm.

When I returned to the barn after my walk, the day's routine was ending. Earl and Rhetta were washing the milking equipment. The cows were finishing the day's last serving of hay and soon would bed down for the night. The sweet stink of the barn rose from our clothes.

At 7 p.m. the lights went off. Dark to dark. Another day's work was done.

Across New England, winter once meant harvesttime. In February or early March, when the ice had thickened and cold still gripped the land, farmers would hike out to their ponds and townsmen would converge on the lakes. It was time to harvest the year's crop of ice. The ice would be scored, sawed, hauled to a storage building, packed in sawdust, and thus preserved for warm-weather use. Ice cutting thrived as an industry from the mid-1800s to the early-1900s. Electric refrigeration then came along, and ice cubes replaced ice blocks. The long handsaws and angular ice plows have been largely forgotten in barns or cataloged in museums. Yet, up in the Green Mountains of Vermont there exists a stream-fed pond where one day every winter the rasp and scrape of an ice harvest can still be heard.

On a bright Saturday in February I met thirty people gathered in the snowbound woods. Most were in high school or college and were outfitted with cross-country skis or snowshoes. One carried three freshly oiled handsaws, about five feet long, with widely spaced teeth, capable, it seemed to me, of cutting down a redwood. The group was affiliated with the Farm and Wilderness Foundation, a Quaker-inspired organization that operates five summer camps in the Green Mountains near Plymouth, Vermont. There is one primitive camp—Flying Cloud—where boys aged 11 through 15 spend the summer in close touch with nature. The campers live in tepees, tend gardens, and practice outdoor survival skills. There is no electricity, hence no refrigeration. So once a year the foundation's alumni, counselors, and administrators make their way to the site of the Flying Cloud camp to cut a summer's supply of ice.

We set out on a trail along the east shoulder of Salt Ash Mountain. The forest, which creaked in the wind like an old house, was primarily beech, with a scattering of birch, spruce, and maple. Through the woods ran the Crown Point Road, a trail connecting the Connecticut River with Lake Champlain. Local tradition says it was used by the Green Mountain Boys during the Revolutionary War.

There was no need to worry about whether the ice was ready. The temperature had fallen to 24 degrees below zero the night before. Two miles up the mountain trail we reached the pond, about 75 feet long and 25 feet across. Early arrivals had started a bonfire for warmth, and others had begun shoveling the four feet of snow that had accumulated on the pond during the winter. During the days of commercial ice cutting, the lakes and ponds were cleared as soon as the ice was thick enough to hold the horses and sleds that would cart the snow away. With the surface clean, the ice froze thicker and faster, and no air bubbles formed to cloud the ice and lessen its appeal. One Vermont firm reportedly gained a reputation for selling ice so clear that a newspaper could be read through a block twenty inches thick.

Once the snow was removed, groups of people took turns serving as "horses," dragging the plow over the ice to make incisions for cutting. (The antique plow and saws had been purchased from an 83-year-old Vermonter.) When the surface had been scored in a checkerboard pattern, the sawing began. Shouts greeted the first block to be extracted. Two feet thick and weighing about 250 pounds, it required several people gripping ice tongs to heft it from the water and haul it fifty feet up an incline to the wooden icehouse.

Old photographs of ice harvests often show curiously dignified men in dark coats and hats standing on frozen lakes with frozen looks. The modern-day group appeared in a spray of colors, in down vests, sweaters, jackets, caps, leggings, and gloves—anything to keep warm. It was too cold to stand around and not work. Beards frosted. A nose started to bleed. One fellow happened to look at Len Cadwallader, the business manager of the foundation, and noticed that his nose had turned white. "Len, your nose is dead," the cutter shouted, and pressed his hands to Len's nose to restore the circulation and prevent frostbite.

Despite the numbing cold, the people threw themselves into the work with as much vigor and enthusiasm as they would for a game of ice hockey. Each harvester acted as if it were his or her fresh-caught fish that would be kept from spoiling the next summer. Ken Webb, who founded the camps with his wife, Susan, in 1939, told me later that their Quaker philosophy inspires the belief that physical work done in cooperation with others enriches the spirit. The people on the pond certainly manifested that belief, seeming to take uncommon delight in the fact that they were working outdoors alongside their friends.

As the afternoon wore on, the dark patch of open water slowly grew. Ice blocks as large as cornerstones were stacked in the shed and covered with sawdust. When about a hundred blocks had been cut and stored, the harvesters packed their tools, snuffed the fire, and skied stiffly back to the road. It had been good to see a near-extinct industry retain a practical application. It was good also to think of the Flying Cloud campers using the ice to keep their food fresh through the summer. Perhaps one might even chisel off a piece and hold it against his brow on a hot afternoon.

Signs of thaw gloriously appeared a few days later as I drove north in Vermont. People with shovels were breaking up the thick gray mats of ice that imprisoned their sidewalks. Brooks began to run. Soon be mud season, noted the farmers. Sap buckets hung from roadside maples. Conversations in taverns turned tremulously to baseball. Yet despite the 40-degree temperature, winter remained. Snow covered the fields, and steel-gray skies drained the landscape of color.

One of the rites of late winter in the northeastern United States is the town meeting, when township citizens gather to elect local officials, approve a budget, and in full-throated expression of their democratic rights, let it be known what they think about any issue that comes to mind. In Vermont the meetings are held on the first Tuesday of March. On the Friday before, photographer Ira Block and I arrived in Craftsbury, about 25 miles south of the Canadian border in the sparsely populated corner of Vermont known as the Northeast Kingdom. The town clerk, preparing to leave for the day, told us that Tuesday's meeting would be interesting. In the lexicon of a Vermonter, "interesting" implies the possibility of high drama.

The township of Craftsbury, with a population of about 750, is made up of several villages and hamlets. Ira and I visited four: Craftsbury (known as the Village), Craftsbury Common (the Common), East Craftsbury, and Collinsville. Like neighborhoods in a large city, each claims a distinct identity. Craftsbury is the commercial quarter. Its main street—one of the few paved streets in town—has two general stores, an auto repair shop, a barbershop, the post office, and the town hall. On Saturday the busiest spot was Raboin's Village Store. While I stood eating a cheese sandwich, a farmer came in to collect 9½ pounds of nails to put up sheathing inside a barn; a grade school girl, sent by her mother, picked up some floral-patterned cloth for a skirt; students from a private school in the Common arrived in a group to cash checks from home; and the principal of the public school system dropped by for a loaf of bread.

My favorite loitering spot came to be the barbershop. I liked the unusual furniture. In the middle of the shop's long, dimly lit front room stood a banquet-size pool table with leather thong pockets. A game of eight ball cost 15 cents. In the small back room, a barber chair faced a mirror and a row of hair-tonic bottles. A Norman Rockwell print of a barbershop was tacked to the wall. That popular American painter, who lived in Vermont, could have used this place as his setting.

The proprietor was Pamphile Beaudoin, a 78-year-old French Canadian known around town as "Barb." He is proud of his "old-fashioned haircuts," the kind that leave a half-moon of skin around the ear. "There's not much business anymore," Barb said, as he worked carefully at repairing a snowshoe. "Ever since people let their hair grow. Used to be people waiting in every seat on a Saturday, and I kept the place open until 11 at night."

It was nearly noon on Saturday when Robert Slicer, a truck driver, became the day's first customer. In his 47 years of clipping in Craftsbury, Barb has tended four generations of Slicers. As Barb circled the chair with his scissors, Robert remembered: "It used to be a big day when I was a kid and could ride my bike to the barbershop, get a haircut, and have a bottle of soda." Haircuts then cost a quarter.

Conversation came slow and lazy, like the dust motes drifting before the window. "What do you think of this warm weather we're having?" "Going to the town meeting on Tuesday?" A couple of boys with hair covering their ears came in from riding their snowmobiles to shoot pool. Barb told them to get a soda from the refrigerator. The smell of hair oil soon signaled that the haircut was about finished. Robert would look neat and trim in the cab of his truck. Barb took his two dollars and returned to the snowshoe. One of the boys put the three ball in a side pocket. I sat by the wood-burning stove, loitering.

East Craftsbury, two miles from Craftsbury, is sometimes called "Miss Jean's town." The name refers to Miss Jean W. Simpson, an 83-year-old millionaire spinster. The Simpson family has lived in the area since 1830 and is the largest landowner in East Craftsbury; the yellow buildings of its Brassknocker dairy farm populate the surrounding countryside. But in the minds of the local citizens, Miss Jean is not known primarily as a wealthy landowner. It is her civic generosity that has made her practically a folk hero.

I met Miss Jean on Sunday morning at the small library she runs in East Craftsbury. Housed in a former country store, the library is a memorial to her father, John Woodruff Simpson, a turn-of-the-century New York lawyer. Small and frail, with two walking sticks within reach, Miss Jean sat at a desk amid books and book reviews and greeted visitors to the library. People arrived throughout the morning, as much to pay her a visit as to check out books. Between guests, she described to me her days as a girl skating in Central Park in New York and how she played Hamlet in a production when no boys were available. But when I asked her about her philanthropy, she jutted her sharp jaw out like a scolding finger and said, "Anyone who has more money than they need should help out." *(Continued on page 31)*
(Continued on page 31)

Craftsbury Township   New England nocturne: Long shadows of late afternoon streak Craftsbury Common, a hilltop hamlet in northern Vermont that boasts both private and

public schools, a post office, and a library. The steepled church and white clapboard homes stand about a mile uphill from the village of Craftsbury. Some 750 people live in the township.

Small-town charms of Craftsbury surface in its long-lived institutions —witch hazel and gossip at the local barbershop (right), familiar strains from a country-music group known as the Eden Mountain Boys (above), and the village's two-room schoolhouse for grades one through three (opposite, upper). Even institutions change, however. Pamphile Beaudoin, better known as "Barb"—the town's only barber for 47 years—retired late in 1979, sold the shop, and moved to New Hampshire.

*D*emocracy takes the stand at a town meeting in Craftsbury, an annual rite of self-government. The elected moderator, Bill Farrar, welcomes townspeople to the hall (left). Exercising his right to dissent, citizen Perley Fielders argues against proposed changes in local fire districting (opposite, lower). A midday break allows Mildred Wells time to lunch and to mull over the issues (below, left) before voting. The final tally (below) finds 97 for, 31 opposed—and Craftsbury commits itself to new fire districting.

The locals are not hesitant to talk about Miss Jean's doings. A former town clerk told me that on several occasions Miss Jean has rescued the school district from financial difficulties with her unadvertised donations. A customer at the barbershop reported that she purchased a van to take schoolchildren to out-of-town sporting events. An innkeeper mentioned that she provided costumes for school plays. Other citizens told me that she holds a corn roast each September at her farm for the schoolchildren and rides in a chariot in the town's Old Home Day parade in August.

Miss Jean did tell me that she "was always too busy to get married." She was most forthcoming, however, when she discussed the artifacts she had collected from around the world. A young couple was peering at some objects in a glass case, and Miss Jean, standing up with difficulty, walked over to tell them about some of the items, such as a bullet found at the Waterloo battlefield, or a pair of Chinese dice cups. "I've always liked collecting things," she told them. "As a girl I would keep a toenail that fell off or a penny that had been run over by a train." She appeared to be successful at collecting friends, as well.

In the foothills a few miles west of the library is Collinsville, a settlement that doesn't appear on many maps. At the turn of the century it was a busy village with a sawmill, a church, and a school, but the mill shut down in 1922 and the population dwindled. Moose are occasionally seen in backyards in the early morning, and at night coyotes wail from the hilltops.

People in the valley sometimes refer to Collinsville residents as "woodchucks"—the New England appellation for hillbillies. Most of the men here make their living as loggers, mechanics, or construction workers. The community of sixty people is intimate, since most members are related by marriage. Griggs, Darling, Waterhouse—the family trees would make a thicket.

On Sunday afternoons the families sometimes get together to play music. Ira and I were invited to one such session at the home of Lawrence Griggs, one of the area's best fiddlers and a regular at the annual Craftsbury Old Time Fiddlers Contest. Young children and their mothers crowded the doorways to the kitchen, while music from three guitars, two banjos, and a fiddle filled the room. Tunes ran from "Your Cheatin' Heart" to "Chattanooga Shoeshine Boy."

Guitarist Allan Maskell excused his scratchy voice: He had celebrated his 30th wedding anniversary the night before. Lawrence Griggs, a short, quiet fellow who never removed his stocking cap, told me that he had learned his fiddling from his mother, a homesteader in Saskatchewan who had met her husband during the wheat harvest. "All the men from here used to go up to the harvest in the fall," Lawrence said. "Four of my father's nine children were born in Saskatchewan." Between songs, Eleanor Griggs, Lawrence's sister-in-law, explained that the musical get-togethers are known in the hills as "kitchen junkets." "Sometimes we bring all the kids, make sandwiches, and people play music while the women chase the kids. A lot of us learned how to square dance at a junket." The band played for about two hours, then

Watery chink in winter's armor, the Deerfield River rolls on near Wilmington in southern Vermont. It passes through national forest lands and feeds reservoirs and power stations on its way to Massachusetts.

voices became hoarse and throats thirsty, and the instruments were packed away. The coyotes on the hilltops would howl on this night.

From outside Collinsville I could look across the Black River to the picturesque hamlet of Craftsbury Common, sitting on a hill of its own. A steepled church—landmark of New England villages—occupies a corner of the green. Handsome white clapboard houses with dark shutters line the main road. Over the years, a muted rivalry has grown up between the Common and the Village. "It is a classic case of top-of-the-hill mentality versus bottom-of-the-hill mentality," observed one Common resident. The Common has the township high school, the Sterling Institute—a private school emphasizing forestry, agriculture, and wildlife management—and a small summer population of well-to-do people from East Coast cities. Consequently, it has traditionally given off a cultured, moneyed air. It has always been regarded as the township's intellectual quarter. The Village is more industrial. Because of this difference in roles, people of the Common have often been accused by Villagers of going around with their noses in the air. The Villagers, in turn, are sometimes thought of by the Commoners as plain. "During my 39 years as township moderator," says Earl Wilson, 75, a lifelong resident of Craftsbury, "I tried to level that hill."

The Vermonter's traditional wariness of outsiders probably accounts for the Village's prejudice. The Common, in many minds, is associated with part-time residents. The number of out-of-staters buying land in the area increases each year. Township officials, however, believe that Craftsbury will not become overwhelmed, as have many towns in the southern half of the state.

Michael and Penny Schmitt are aware that they are thought of as outsiders. Frequent summer visitors to the area, the Schmitts in 1973 bought a vacation mansion in the Common and turned it into an inn. Michael and Penny had been successful professionals in New York City, but like most immigrants to Vermont they desired the country life full time. "You have to learn to quiet up when you first move into a small town," Penny said, curled up on a couch in the inn's front room. "The single biggest mistake made by outsiders is to throw their weight around, trying to impress the locals with a different set of values."

Because they believe the township is being run competently, Michael and Penny have stayed in the background of local affairs. Michael, however, hopes that the town will someday make use of them. "My only criticism is that Penny and I are young and ambitious, and we represent transferable assets that haven't been pressed into service. Perhaps it's a failing of the town that it isn't encouraging this." Penny, who is a direct descendant of Ethan Allen, said that for the time being they will accept their status as "permanent summer people." She added: "Nothing happens quickly here, but that's why it works so well."

On Tuesday morning trucks and automobiles lined the main street of Craftsbury. It was town meeting day, time for the citizens to have a say in the workings of the township. The windows of the wooden town hall quickly fogged up as about 150 of the local citizens came out of a cold rain and settled onto folding chairs. Schools had been closed, and a few children, probably instructed by their teachers to attend and observe democracy in action, looked on from the balcony. On the stage sat the town officials and a coffeepot.

At ten sharp the crack of a gavel began the meeting. Moderator

Bill Farrar, looking somewhat out of place in his sport coat and tie, handled business with the briskness of an auctioneer. "What's your pleasure?" he called, as he opened nominations for candidates to town offices. A quick smile or an offhand remark greeted the election of candidates. The excitement came whenever someone on the floor called for a ballot vote. The noise would begin abruptly, like the chatter of insects as darkness falls. Chairs scraped and voices buzzed as the citizens filed up the aisles and dropped their ballots into a box. No one checked registration; town clerk Neil Goodwin knew everyone personally. Votes were counted on the spot, and the meeting proceeded.

During the course of the day, citizens stood up and spoke forcefully about such issues as enforcing the dog ordinance (a reference to packs of domestic dogs that were running down deer); or finding a clean-up committee for the fiddlers' contest; or whether a full-time librarian and guidance counselor were needed for the schools. My years in Washington, D.C., had not prepared me for the honesty, the restrained behavior, the absence of statistics, and the informality of the Vermonters. In one instance a man's word swung the vote. Moderator Farrar, as a director of the water company in Craftsbury Common, had proposed that the Common establish itself as a fire district separate from the rest of the township so it could raise capital on its own to salvage the aging water facility. The idea did not sit well. "Why don't the Common people drill wells like everyone else," asked a farmer. Another said, "*I've* never had to ask for state help." Perley Fielders, a Craftsbury innkeeper who three years before had returned to Vermont after living for a time in Washington, D.C., stood up, waved a book of statutes, and, with the fervor of a prosecuting attorney, warned that "the Common will become a separate political entity and will be able to raise taxes. This would change the character of Craftsbury."

With the argument heating up and the outcome of the vote in doubt, Farrar took the floor again. After promising that the people outside the Common would not be taxed for any repairs to the water plant, Farrar declared in a voice taut with sincerity, "You're raising fears that don't exist. I've lived in Craftsbury all my life, and as long as I'm here, it won't change." Someone called for a vote. The tally: 97 yes, 31 no. The Common became a new fire district.

I remarked later to Neil Goodwin that I thought Perley had been convincing. "Yes, he made a nice plea," Neil said. "But Perley's too new. He doesn't talk the farmers' language. It makes a difference."

So the meeting went on. The PTA sold sandwiches. Miss Jean Simpson won approval for another Old Home Day celebration. (Sadly, it would be her last; Miss Jean died early in 1980.) "Barb" Beaudoin stayed home. One of the Waterhouse men from Collinsville was defeated in an election for selectman. And Michael Schmitt found himself arguing publicly in favor of the new fire districting. At 2:15 the meeting adjourned, and the main street of Craftsbury became deserted again. The township would carry on for another year.

The next morning I headed east toward Maine. Two high school boys playing pool at the barbershop had told me that anytime you can hear the train in Hardwick, eight miles away, it means the weather will be rainy the next day. The whistle must have moaned loudly that night, for the rain didn't quit for a week. When I reached southern Maine, it had washed the snow away. I felt disoriented. Every day for a month I had seen crisp vistas of white (Continued on page 41)

Maine North Country

Wall of newly delivered spruce and fir logs dwarfs Harold Pelletier as he calculates its volume for payment. Trucked to this railhead at St. John, the 1,500 cords shown here will travel south by train to a

pulp-and-paper mill at Jay. Forest products provide 30 percent of the jobs in the Pine Tree State, especially in northern areas such as Fort Kent (below, right). Many loggers, including Joe Lagacé (bottom), cross over from Canada to work for firms in the U.S.

Monhegan Island   Bereft of summer tourists and seasonal residents, this
island *12* miles off the coast of Maine weathers another winter, engaging in its established

mainstay—lobstering. The season runs from January through June. The island's squat hotel, deserted and boarded up, faces a bay where fishing boats ride at anchor.

*S*imple pleasures such as mussels and beer, savored in a warm fish house (left), team up with plenty of hard work for bearded lobsterman Sherman Stanley, Jr. From his boat Northwind (above), he checks in one day perhaps 150 lobster pots. The fifty legal-size lobsters—or keepers—he caught this day represent a "mediocre" catch, he says. If not sold at once, they go into a floating wooden crate (far right). At day's end, Sherman beaches a skiff (right) with helper Leslie Whitney, one of Monhegan's few lobsterwomen.

Tools of the lobstering trade—buoys, netting, poles, boots, slickers, and **41**
more—surround Sherman Stanley and his father in Sherman's fish house.
Traditionally all-male enclaves, fish houses provide places for repairing gear,
cutting bait, or waiting out bad weather with a marathon game of cribbage.

fields and dark trees. In Maine the grass was the color of straw, and the
trees looked drab without a backdrop of snow. The landscape had lost
its grandeur. The color that finally attracted me was the blue of the
ocean, sighted near Rockland.

For the next few days I meandered along the coast, trying to keep
the water in sight. One morning in a little resort town on a peninsula
poking into Penobscot Bay, I walked into a corner variety store and
found a clutch of local men at the counter matching quarters over
coffee. They were chattering busily, belying the taciturn image of New
Englanders. Edging into the conversation, I asked if there was any
fishing going on in the area. "Over on the island of Monhegan," one
fellow said. "They fish for lobster in winter. Have to. They can't after
June." Within a few days I was a passenger on a mail boat out of Port
Clyde, on my way to Monhegan, 12 miles out to sea.

The arrival of the mail boat in winter is a social occasion on the tiny
island, which has an area of less than one square mile. When I stepped
ashore, nearly a third of the ninety year-round residents had gathered
at the dock to greet passengers, help unload supplies, and check the
mail. The number of people on hand was particularly high because the
lobstermen had stayed ashore. The wind was blowing at 25 to 40 knots;
whitecapped waves surged through the water. The sea was too rough.

The Maine lobsterman is a romantic figure in the American
imagination: a weather-hardened man in a spray-flecked yellow
slicker, pulling up his catch while battling a tempestuous sea.
During my visit, the lobstermen wisely weren't interested in battling the
tempestuous sea. They were waiting out a spell of bad weather. They
have had to deal with winter seas since 1907, when the island petitioned
the state legislature to limit lobster fishing near Monhegan to a Janu-
ary-through-June season. The conservation-minded community did
not want its waters depleted of its main cash crop. Islanders chose the
winter and spring months because the lobsters are then at their
meatiest. Lobsters shed their shells in summer to grow and breed and
are not as desirable in this condition. Also, lobsters in winter fetch the
highest price. Monhegan remains the one place in the United States
that has voluntarily instituted a lobster season.

When the lobstermen aren't at sea, they sit in their fish houses,
usually tending equipment. One day I was visiting the fish house of
Sherman Stanley, Jr., when six or seven other fishermen dropped by to
grouse and gossip. Inside the shed, buoys hung from the ceiling like
plants, new rope was coiled on the floor, and tools were strewn on a
workbench. On the wall hung pinups, and liquor bottles were stashed
on several shelves. The fish house is a man's club; the language is salty,
and shoptalk prevails. While Sherman worked on a new wire lobster
trap, the talk turned to expenditures: how much the traps wrecked in
the bad weather would cost; how much the government takes in taxes;
how much boat repairs go for. A bottle of rum was passed around. I was
surprised at how young the fishermen were. Of the 14 on the island,

St. Regis Indian Reservation

Mohawk medicine man Myron Clute displays some of the dozens of herbs he collects, dries, and prescribes for various physical and mental complaints. Lobelia—Indian tobacco—sumac berries, wild cherry bark, ginseng, even corn silk, possess curative powers, he believes. A traditionalist, Myron still practices some ancient longhouse rituals at the reservation in upstate New York.

almost all are in their 20s or 30s. About a third are former summer
residents who decided to stay. Many courted and married women who
also had come over for the summer season.

A sense of fraternity exists in the fishing community. According to
tradition, if one man is sick on January 1, the opening day of the season,
the rest wait for him to get well. That way, everyone can set his traps on
the same day. "We generally follow that line of thinking," said Sherman's father, Sherman Stanley, Sr. "Twice since 1946 we've waited as
late as January 14. A cut foot and a case of flu were the reasons."

The wind relented one day, and the lobstermen donned their
slickers and ventured out to check their traps. I joined Sherman Jr. on
his 35-foot *Northwind*. A hefty, bearded fellow in his mid-30s, Sherman
is the third generation of Stanleys to fish off Monhegan. He has a wife
named Ruth and two children—a toddler-daughter named Adair and a
son, Dwight. His colleagues describe him as a "high liner"—a Maine
accolade for a top fisherman. For most of the day we cruised within two
miles of the island in ten to twenty fathoms of water. Buoys of different
colors, the property of individual fishermen, bobbed in the water like
beads, signaling the location of the bottom-lying traps. Sherman sets
600 traps, the island limit, and hauls a quarter of them a day.

We quickly established a routine. "I see a big lobster grinning up at
me," Sherman would announce as he winched up a trap. He would
fling each lobster onto a table, where Leslie Whitney, one of the few
women on Monhegan to work on lobster boats, would measure it,
looking for a "keeper"—a lobster with a carapace, or top shell, between
3³⁄₁₆ and 5 inches long. Lobsters that were too short or too long she
would toss back into the water.

Leslie also filled the traps with fresh bait of herring and redfish
heads, and—amid swirls of carping gulls—shoved them back into the
sea to be checked again in four days. Our biggest catch was a three-
pounder. Sherman imagined the scene: "That will cost thirty dollars in
a restaurant. Probably some politician in Washington will buy it."

Sherman didn't keep any lobsters for himself. At $3.75 a pound he
couldn't afford to, he said. In the summer the price slides to $1.50 a
pound. We hauled close to 140 traps during the day and found about
fifty worthy lobsters—a mediocre catch, according to Sherman, who
speculated that the lobsters weren't moving around the bottom in such
cold weather. By day's end Sherman and Leslie were tired from hauling
and baiting. As for me, I was nearly exhausted merely from bracing my
feet on deck all day in the choppy water and trying to keep my breakfast
down. A southerly blew in overnight, and the lobstermen were back in
the fish houses next day, griping and joking. That day I saw a fan of
Canada geese fly over the island, forecasting spring. It was nowhere in
sight on Monhegan.

After leaving Monhegan, I turned north again and drove through
Maine's up-country. I was beginning to feel like a migratory animal
myself, moving steadily across the land, stopping only briefly. The
difference, of course, is that migratory creatures have a definite route.
I often didn't know where I would be going the next day.

As I drew inland, forests of pine, spruce, and fir began to crowd
the roads, continuing unbroken at times for thirty or forty miles. Cities
announced themselves with clouds of steam billowing from pulp-and-
paper mills. In Aroostock County, highway signs promised moose, but
I saw none. Trucks stacked with fifty-foot logs rushed around corners

like juggernauts. Timber operators were hurrying to beat the spring thaw that would turn the logging roads into quagmires.

At Fort Kent—where U.S. Route 1 ends after its 2,362-mile run north from Key West, Florida—I crossed the St. John River and entered Canada. I indulged in a trucker's day, driving headlong for 450 miles through Quebec Province, pulling off the road only to eat and buy fuel. At Montreal I swung south and reentered the United States in eastern New York. Weary from driving, I halted just inside the border at the St. Regis Indian Reservation, home to 7,000 Mohawk Indians.

Minuscule compared with reservations in the West, the St. Regis settlement covers 37½ square miles, two-thirds of it in Canada. I visited the small museum on the American side and, amid the headdresses and baskets made of ash splints and sweet grass, saw a collection of masks, their expressions grotesque, as if modeled in some hell. Noses were bent, mouths twisted or swollen, eyes wide and maniacal. The curator, Martha La France, told me that the faces represented mythical beings, known as the False Faces, who live in the woods and possess healing powers. These masks were copies; thirty originals, carved from living trees, are stored away and used twice a year in healing ceremonies. I had thought that the role of the medicine man had declined in most Indian cultures, but Martha shook her head. "A lot of people on this reservation are treated by medicine men for alcoholism or sicknesses that have no cause. If you believe you'll be healed, you'll be healed." At my urging she agreed to ask a medicine man if he would talk with me.

That afternoon I met Myron Clute in the library. Appearing to be about 40, he had a strong, athletic face and wore his long, gray-flecked hair in a ponytail. At first he seemed reluctant to speak to an outsider about his role as a medicine man. He preferred to talk, in hushed library tones, about his hopes for the revival of traditional Mohawk life. He wanted to reinstate the longhouse as the axis of social life. Sensing that my interest was genuine, Myron began to open up. He told me that he was regularly treating "a few" people in St. Regis. "In some cases, I tell them to get X rays or a diagnosis from a white doctor so they can find out what's wrong. Then they can come back and look at the herbs." Myron showed me a photo album with color snapshots of the medicinal herbs found in the area. "Tea brewed from sumac berries can cure swollen gums, and goldenseal can control diarrhea," he said. "The medicine man must understand that with these herbs it is like he is dealing with a person. He must be able to capture the spirit of the plant and release it at the right time."

Myron also believes that disease can be spirit-induced. "I was once brought a young guy I thought was crazy," Myron said. "He was coughing and he kept grabbing at his throat, as if something was inside. I felt what seemed to be a pencil, but whenever I touched it the object went limp. I made him some medicine, a special brew, and the next day he was all right." I asked Myron for his diagnosis. "I believe it was the result of a grudge felt by another Indian."

Shortly before dusk Myron asked if I'd like to make a call with him. We drove to the fringe of the community, to the home of a preacher at the longhouse. Myron explained that the man was "troubled by spirits." The patient didn't appear to have anything wrong as he described how Indian medicine once saved his life after a broken rib had punctured his heart. When the man's wife and two children came into the room, Myron pulled out a leather pouch of tobacco and asked me, as a

Lebanon Valley   *Veterinarian George Keck serves dairy farms in rural Pennsylvania. One tranquilized patient, lashed and padded for her own safety, undergoes corrective postpartum surgery (above). Drawers of medical supplies make George's carryall (below) a mobile hospital; a two-way radio inside the vehicle keeps him informed of emergencies while on the road.*

Middle Creek Wildlife Management Area   *Dusk flight of Canada
geese wings over a man-made lake in Pennsylvania. The preserve, put together from marsh and*

farmland in 1966 to attract waterfowl, now provides a year-round home for 4,000 geese and a winter stopover for 30,000 more migrating along the Atlantic flyway.

*W*ary-eyed goose hisses a warning to intruders from atop her rubber-tire nest at Middle Creek (left); a second honker spreads its wings in a threat display (below, right). If badly irritated, geese will attack animals much larger than themselves. Nesting begins in late winter as pairs (above) grow increasingly territorial. Some build nests from sticks and grasses (below, left); others prefer the old tires, metal drums, or other artificial nests. Grain planted on high ground helps sustain large nesting populations of ducks— mallards, blacks, pintails, and wood ducks—as well as the geese.

Winter's wane puts a spring in the step of Amish girls visiting Middle Creek on a mild Sunday afternoon. The wildlife area's nearness and noncommercial nature make it popular among Lancaster County's Amish and Mennonite families, who sometimes come here to ramble, picnic, or play softball or volleyball. Hewing to simple and unworldly ways, these neighborly people—many of them farmers—still feel a closeness to the land that most other Americans lost long ago.

non-Indian, to wait in the next room. I soon heard him chanting in the nasal voice the Mohawks attribute to the False Faces, and I could smell tobacco burning. Indian tobacco is sacred to the Mohawks: The smoke is thought to carry messages to the Creator. After a few minutes I was called back and asked to sit down at what Myron called a "death feast," to celebrate the dispelling of the injurious spirit. The meal was plain—chicken, potatoes, and beans—and conversation was carried on as if nothing had happened. Afterward, Myron explained that the tobacco-burning ritual relieved depression. "What you heard but did not see," Myron said, "was Indian psychiatry at work."

Most Indians on the reservation believe in the benefits of herbal medicines, I was told, but only a few take the time to prepare and use them. One day while watching Agnes Garrow, an elderly Indian woman, weave a basket, I complained of a stiff neck. She said she had

something to help and went into the kitchen. I imagined her making a paste out of herbs and was excited at the prospect of trying an Indian medicine. She reappeared shortly and handed me a bottle of Absorbine Junior muscle liniment.

Down in southern Pennsylvania several days later I met another man of medicine, one who often ties up his patients, doesn't ask them how they feel, prescribes pills as large as knuckles, and washes his boots after each visit. He is George Keck, a farm-animal veterinarian. I spent a few days with George in Lebanon County, east of Harrisburg, and learned quite a bit about the anatomy of a milk cow. On one typical day George made 11 barn calls: He assisted at births; checked a herd of Charolais cattle to see which were ready for breeding; examined two cases of sore feet; treated cows for diarrhea and mastitis (inflammation of the mammary gland); injected a calcium solution into a cow down with milk fever; surveyed a herd of Holsteins for signs of tuberculosis; gave flu shots to a pen of calves; and treated a heifer for warts. Eleven times he washed the barnyard muck off his boots.

George, 50, has been spending his days like this for twenty years. He works within a 15-to-20-mile radius of his home in Annville and drives some 35,000 miles a year in a four-wheel-drive truck. His wife takes calls at home and radios them to him in the vehicle. "Late winter is the busiest time of the year," George said as we drove down a narrow road. "The rush will last until the first cutting of hay in June. The cattle are still in the barns, and the farmers want them to get worked on."

The countryside we drove through was restful and rolling, dotted with small farms whose silver-capped silos glinted warmly in the sun. Some farmers had begun to turn their fields, and the deep brown of the soil contrasted vividly with the muted, late-winter hues. Blackbirds and gulls scavenged in the fresh earth. Many of the farms we visited had been owned by the same family for two or more generations. The homes were built of the milky gray limestone that appears in outcroppings throughout Lebanon Valley. The farmers speak in lilting tones that reflect their German ancestry.

A barn visit by George costs eight dollars plus the cost of medicine, breeding tests (fifty cents a head), or operations. To examine a cow that had lost its appetite, to provide pills and shots, and to administer pregnancy tests, George charged one farmer $29. Two visits, medicine, and an operation for a twisted stomach cost another man $80. George guessed that he makes half the money of a general practitioner. Horse vets and small-animal doctors with clinics also take in more. "I'd rather work with a dairyman, though. He's a practical businessman," George said as we walked out of a barn into a light snowfall. (Local farmers call a late-winter dusting "zwivvele schnee"—onion snow—because onion sprouts have already broken ground in the gardens.) "The dairyman is with his cows all day," George went on. "A horse owner in these parts might not see his animals till the end of the day or on weekends. I like dairymen. I enjoy helping them make a profit."

The one major operation I observed was for a twisted stomach—a condition that sometimes afflicts cows after labor. George performs as many as five of these operations a week. This one took place in an old, high-ceilinged barn, cold and dim. To work on the patient, George drugged it with a tranquilizer and had it turned on its back. Its hind legs were tied to a roof beam, its front legs chained to a post, and its snout roped to a stall gate. The setup resembled a medieval torture rig. Bales of hay were packed around the cow to restrain it if it struggled. Working briskly and confidently, George shaved the cow's abdomen and made an incision just large enough for his hand. The farmer, Russell Heilman, stood silently near the cow's head, a mournful look on his face. George's hand searched inside the cow, feeling its four-chambered stomach. "There's the rumen, the second section," he said softly, as if to himself. "Ah, there's the reticulum, the first compartment. Okay, I feel the abomasum; that's the fourth part, and it *is* displaced."

The operation presented a peculiar scene: a doctor in gray coveralls kneeling beside an overturned cow, his hand roaming inside it, breezily relating a story about another operation that had made a neighboring farmer's son sick; two farmhands standing in the gloom of the barn, hands jammed in pockets, mesmerized; a row of cows peering out from between the slats of a stall; six mischievous piglets scampering around the doctor's black bag. "Got it," George finally said. He sutured the stomach muscle back in its proper place, then stitched up the flesh and skin. When the ropes and chains were loosened, the cow wobbled to its feet and walked into its stall, where it stared blankly at the wall. "You can milk her this evening," George said. Then he washed his boots and disappeared down the road.

Winter was ending. I could see the tilt of the season in trees dusted with green and brooks running fast with melted snow. I rolled down the window and stuck out an elbow, content to spend a day aimlessly driving through the lovely farm country. Near Schaefferstown I heard a honking in the sky. I looked up and saw a formation of Canada geese passing overhead. This seemed odd. They had supposedly left their wintering grounds near Chesapeake Bay a month ago, in early March. I assumed that I had just seen the season's last stragglers, but a hundred yards farther along I came to a corner of a field where dozens of geese clustered around a pond, their long black necks bent to the ground as they fed. A sign read "Middle Creek Wildlife Management Area." I turned down a side road, and everywhere I looked were more geese, thick as crows in the stubbly cornfields, unperturbed by my presence. I wanted to shout my excitement. Back roads always offer the possibility of stumbling upon wildlife. I had seen no moose in Maine, but here in rural Pennsylvania, expecting nothing beyond a spring robin, I discovered fields teeming with wild geese.

At the visitor center, manager Charlie Strouphar told me that the preserve, with 5,000 acres of fields and ponds, was started in 1966 by the Pennsylvania Game Commission to attract geese flying south on the Atlantic flyway. The Commission also hoped to retain a year-round population. The preserve has been successful on both counts. In winter as many as 30,000 geese have stopped here, and another 4,000 live in the area the entire year. The preserve also attracts other waterfowl, such as swans from the Yukon and Northwest Territories, and a large number of ducks, mostly mallards, blacks, pintails, and wood ducks.

As Charlie showed me the grounds, we witnessed vivid signs that winter was waning. Across the fields geese were pairing up. A couple broke off from a feeding crowd and, with stately waddles, wandered away. We even spied several females on nests. One was behind a blackberry briar. "It's hugging the ground like a snake, thinking no one will see it," Charlie said. Its mate was drifting in a nearby pond, ready to protect the nest from intruders: raccoons, foxes, writers.

At sunset I stationed myself at a point of land near the man-made lake. As the sky to the east purpled, a skein of ducks, their wings pumping fast, crossed the lake to the woods. Then, shortly after six o'clock, with the sun falling behind a ridge, a great noise filled the sky. Hundreds and hundreds of geese were returning to the lake for the night. There were no patterns, so great was the number of wheeling birds. The noise was loud, chaotic, and wild.

I stood on the shore, entranced. The wild birds reminded me of other woods and lakes where you can free yourself from the cares of daily life and exist, if only for a short time, in the midst of the unpredictable and the grand. Darkness soon fell, and the sky emptied. A stillness washed over the lake. In the distance I saw tracers of light— cars on the Pennsylvania Turnpike. At this hour movement belonged once again to the highways. I continued my own migration.

Spring

ON AN APRIL NIGHT in the Virginia countryside, a single light burned in a barn outside Gainesville. Five people stood huddled like surgeons before a stall where Copper Jewel had dropped to her side in the straw. The mare's belly was swollen, her breathing slow and harsh. From her hindquarters a small brown leg protruded. At a signal from Michael Flynn, manager of the farm, two young women—stable hands—gripped the leg carefully and pulled, to the push of the mare's pelvic muscles. Slowly a second leg emerged, followed by a tiny head, the eyes still shut, a pink tongue sticking out of the mouth like the point of a handkerchief. Another pull and out slid the rib cage. The creature took its first breath. The large eyes opened. A horse had been born.

I watched the proceedings in churchly silence, having never before witnessed a birth. A newborn Thoroughbred looks to be all legs, and the legs of this one tangled and buckled for nearly an hour before it managed a wobbly balance. Copper Jewel nudged the foal toward her flank and soon a loud gurgling was heard. "It must be like a long drink of cold beer in the middle of summer," Michael Flynn said. The next morning the colt was racing around a field like a wild deer.

Thus my spring began. A few days earlier I had shelved my cold-weather gear in Washington, D.C., and resumed my circuit of the United States in Virginia's horse country in the north-central part of the state. White rail fences line the roads here. Horses bend their necks to feed in the greening pastures. Mansions sit on hilltops, partially veiled by trees. The landscape is a tableau of gentility.

I had pulled my van onto the grounds of the Marsh Thoroughbred Farm near Gainesville, having heard that several mares were ready to foal. Copper Jewel, the one expected to deliver next, was still complacently chewing her oats, though now more than two weeks overdue. I decided to wait. In the meantime I tagged along with Michael Flynn, a bearded Irishman from County Tipperary. The 340-acre farm, owned by John D. Marsh, has a single purpose: raising racehorses. In its ten years of operation the farm has been "reasonably successful," according to Michael, who also trains the horses. Majesty's World, the farm's most successful racer thus far, won $119,000 in 1979. Another horse, Eager Exchange, ran in the 1972 Preakness. The farm carries 50 to 75 horses, including all the broodmares, yearlings, and foals. Of this number, Michael was readying 16 for the racetrack later in the spring. Though the all-important bloodlines of the farm's horses are first-rate, Michael admits that none of the 16 are of a caliber to win the Kentucky Derby, or any other important race.

While I made the rounds with Michael—feeding the pregnant mares, letting the yearlings out to frisk in the fields, exercising the racehorses—I marveled at the pampered life of a Thoroughbred. I

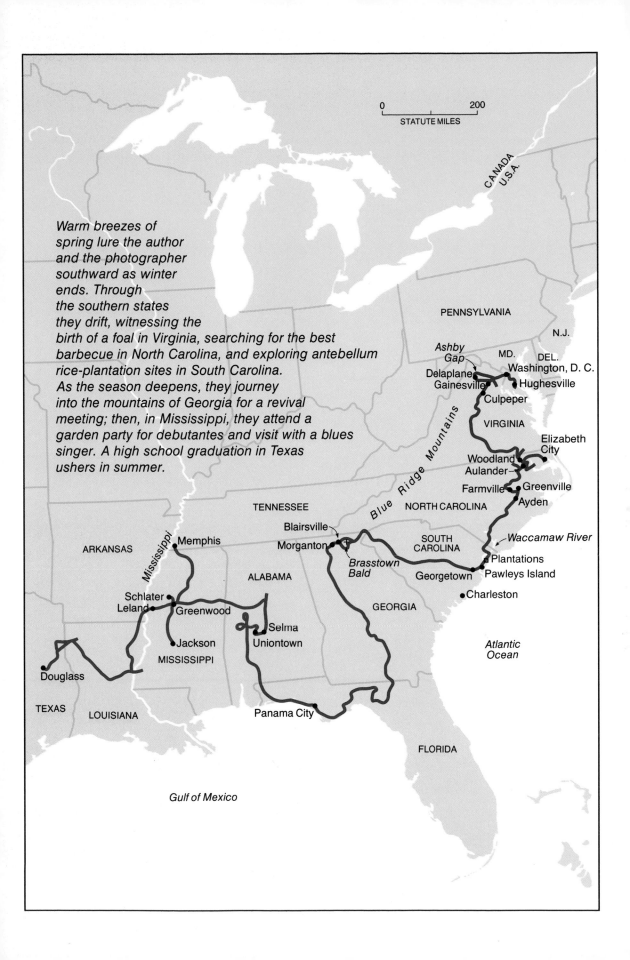

Warm breezes of
spring lure the author
and the photographer
southward as winter
ends. Through
the southern states
they drift, witnessing the
birth of a foal in Virginia, searching for the best
barbecue in North Carolina, and exploring antebellum
rice-plantation sites in South Carolina.
As the season deepens, they journey
into the mountains of Georgia for a revival
meeting; then, in Mississippi, they attend a
garden party for debutantes and visit with a blues
singer. A high school graduation in Texas
ushers in summer.

0   200
STATUTE MILES

CANADA
U.S.A.

PENNSYLVANIA

N.J.

Ashby
Gap   MD.   DEL.
Delaplane   Washington, D. C.
Gainesville   Hughesville
              Culpeper
                        VIRGINIA

Blue Ridge Mountains

Elizabeth
City
Woodland
Aulander
Farmville   Greenville
Ayden

TENNESSEE

Blairsville   NORTH CAROLINA
Morganton

Waccamaw River

SOUTH
CAROLINA

Brasstown
Bald   Georgetown

Memphis

ARKANSAS

Plantations
Pawleys Island

Charleston

ALABAMA   GEORGIA

Schlater
Leland   Greenwood
              Selma
              Uniontown
Jackson

Atlantic
Ocean

Mississippi

MISSISSIPPI

Douglass

TEXAS   LOUISIANA

Panama City

FLORIDA

Gulf of Mexico

Ashby Gap *Flowering dogwoods herald spring's welcome arrival in the foothills of the Blue Ridge Mountains six miles north of Delaplane, Virginia. Early morning fog rises*

*from pond and stream and settles in hollows of the rich, rolling farmland. In the distance, twin
ridges of Lost Mountain, gentled by ages of erosion, rise a thousand feet.*

kept thinking of the dark, cold cow barns I had seen in New England in February. There the animals, though carefully looked after, were nonetheless regarded essentially as valuable machines. Here the stable hands keep the stalls practically spotless. They attend to a horse's slightest physical discomfort and croon to a temperamental steed as if it were a prima donna. "A cow is a mere producer," Michael said. "A Thoroughbred is an athlete." A Thoroughbred is also an extremely valuable property. A good registered milk cow may sell for up to $7,000. Marsh sold a young broodmare last year for $150,000.

My favorite time of the day came when Michael worked the horses at the farm's private half-mile dirt track. Standing in a small viewing stand, a stopwatch in his hand, Michael stared intently at the horses as they sped down the track. Although there was no grandstand and no roaring crowd, no line of numbers flashing on a board and no announcer's voice soaring into incomprehensibility, I still felt a surge of excitement as I watched the blur of muscle and mane as the horses pounded down the stretch and swept across the finish line.

For the three- and four-year-old horses, veterans of the racetrack, Michael was concerned primarily with getting them in shape after their winter layoff. He wanted to see their bellies tighten and their strides lengthen. When the two-year-olds came on the track, Michael shifted his concern to mental conditioning. These horses had never raced before, and he wanted to build up their will and desire, those delicate qualities that make a racehorse great. He ordered the riders to hold the horses back as they ran. "They're like kids," he observed, as Where's Smoky and Delta Fleet tore away from the starting pole. "You don't want to hurt their feelings. Let them think, 'I could have won if the jockey had let me loose.' In a couple of months we'll begin to really race them and find out who's fastest."

A few moments later the two horses completed their quarter-mile sprint, coming in at the finish in a dead heat. Michael was excited now. "I like to see that," he cried. "Ears pricked, mouths open, pushing hard, saying, 'Let's go, let's go.' I'm very pleased."

By the time Copper Jewel finally dropped her foal, near midnight on a Saturday, I too had been touched by the optimism that rules a horse farm in the spring. Foals are being born; the two-year-olds are discovering their racing legs; the older horses are prepping for another season at the track. There are no losers at this time of year. Dreams come naturally.

After the birth, when Michael and the other spectators began drifting out of the barn, I lingered to gaze at the splay-legged foal, much smaller than a carousel animal, and I imagined how it would look in the winner's circle. A stable hand, laying down a new bed of straw, noticed that the newborn horse wore a distinctive snip of white on its forehead. Turning to no one in particular, pitchfork in hand, she announced, "He will be an easily recognized Derby champion."

Below Culpeper, colors began to assert themselves as I drove south: the red clay of plowed fields, the green of high pastures, the white and pink shimmer of dogwoods, the yellow of field grass. In the small towns I passed through, the street activity on Sunday afternoons centered on the self-service car wash, where men wiped and buffed their autos to a shine. Rainstorms came and went.

When I reached eastern North Carolina, I began to think about going fishing. It seemed that at least half of the conversations I had had

Marsh Thoroughbred Farm *Three-week-old foal faces the world with assurance—as long as its mother stands near. Now spindly, his legs may one day carry the colors of the farm, located near Gainesville, Virginia, into the winner's circle.*

*F*lying *hooves kick up a cloud of dirt as Palace and Bold Fencer, neck and neck at the 16th pole, head down the home stretch. With lengthening days and warmer weather, Marsh Thoroughbred Farm begins training two-year-olds such as these for the racing circuit. Exercise riders run the animals at a gallop every morning; about once a week they "breeze" them—let them race each other at a fast but not furious pace. After their run, three Thoroughbreds stand in an equine whirlpool bath (right) under the watchful eye of rider Pattie Powell. The bath cools the horses' legs and reduces inflammation. Mares and their foals (above) laze in a pasture bright with April sunlight.*

with people on the back roads had turned to tales of hunting and fishing. Southerners appeared to be particularly eager sportsmen. That fishing is a venerable pastime in the South was made evident when I picked up the Raleigh *News and Observer* and read a high-flown editorial on the matter. "If a man is ever to find peace, he need not look past a shaded river bank," the editor intoned. "And, may the benevolent gods be praised, he no longer has to lie or make flimsy excuses for taking off from pretty working weather to indulge his soul along the purling waters." Excuses, begone then! The sun was warm, the sky clear, and water was probably purling somewhere nearby.

I found a partner in Herbert Jenkins, Jr. Herbert lives for quail hunting, but he doesn't need any excuses to go fishing, either. He took me to his secret creek in the marshy tidewater country near Albemarle Sound south of Elizabeth City. A reserved, white-haired man in his sixties who lives in Aulander, Herbert began coming to this favorite fishing hole in the mid-1940s. After 1952, the demands of his fertilizer and tobacco businesses, together with the death of a close fishing buddy, led him to give up fishing for 25 years. It took a coronary bypass operation to persuade him to cut back on the work and to bring him back to the creek.

Herbert is a flycaster. No hook-baiting and long, still waits for him. "I like to see that fish hit my fly on top of the water," he told me. We traveled half a mile down the black-water creek in his small outboard, then drifted toward a bank where, among tall moss-hung cypress trees and assorted logs and stumps, the bass and bream were allegedly waiting. My only previous use of a fly rod had been during a slapstick night on a drainage ditch in western Montana. That didn't count.

"Bring the rod back to one o'clock," Herbert instructed me. "Pause for the line to straighten, then flick the rod forward and downward." I needed most of the afternoon just to become slightly competent. (I stopped snagging the line in the moss on every other cast.) Often I just sat in the bow and admired my partner's technique as he sent the line whistling softly across the still water, landing it impeccably a foot from the desired stump.

Just as I began to grow discouraged and was content to sit and enjoy the scenery, my line jumped. I sprang to my feet and began reeling it in. "Play with him, let him run, and have yourself some fun," Herbert advised. "As my old friend said, 'It may be your last.'" I allowed the fish a few bursts of energy, but then, impatient to see whatever was straining on the other end, I pulled in the line and found a thrashing one-and-a-half-pound bass, the largest fish I had ever caught. Proud of myself, I was eager to catch more.

For the next hour I rarely averted my eyes from the white fly floating on the surface. Meanwhile, Herbert and I took turns sounding profound on the habits of fish. We speculated endlessly on why the fish wouldn't bite at a certain spot, why they stayed close to wood, why they had hit on an afternoon five days earlier but not now. Fish became the most fascinating and stimulating subject imaginable. Habits, emotions, ideas, virtues, vices: All were attributed by us to our quarry. "They're mischievous." "No, they're bored." "Maybe just shy." "Oh, this one's a shrewd one." "He's frightened." "They're mocking us!"

By light's end Herbert and I had thrown a fair mess of fish into the cooler. I remembered that, during the drive to the creek, I had nearly

*Lazy day in Virginia draws regulars to the porch of the Delaplane Store, built
in 1852 and now run by a descendant of an early owner.*

asked Herbert why he liked fishing. It would have been a foolish
question. The reasons unfolded with the afternoon: the hush, the
unwinding, the drifting hours sparked by anticipation, the late afternoon light burning the water into a perfect mirror. We spotted a water
moccasin wrapped around a stump and a family of three otters sporting in a patch of lily pads. We heard coon dogs baying and watched
wood ducks flying overhead. We caught several fish and became
friends. A very foolish question.

I didn't stay with Herbert long enough to taste the fish we had
hooked. Instead, on the following morning, I climbed back into my van
and devoted the day to a search for the best barbecue in eastern North
Carolina. People had been urging me to taste this local food, as if a
helping would emblazon the memory of North Carolina on both my
mind and my stomach. So I asked some fellows at a corner gas station in
Saratoga where I could find good barbecue. A short, sharp-featured
man in grease-coated clothes looked up and said, "Parkers in Greenville. It's the best in the state." This began the argument. The subject of

barbecue, though not commanding quite the strident emotions accorded college basketball in North Carolina, certainly inspires raised voices. The main point of contention seemed to be that the chef at Parkers cooks his pork in gas-heated pits, while the more traditional (and more flavorful, according to one vociferous camp) barbecue is made over the coals of an oak-wood fire.

I broke in to ask where I could find the wood-cooked variety. "There's a great place in Farmville," I was told.

I drove ten miles to Farmville and stopped at another gas station for directions. The attendant allowed that, indeed, good barbecue was available in town, but that I could find an even better place in Ayden. "They both do it the old way—over wood—but," and here the man lowered his voice confidentially, "the Ayden man don't grind his meat. There's a difference."

The tiny restaurant by the railroad tracks in Farmville turned out to be closed for the day, so I left for Ayden, 15 miles away. Coming to a country store, I asked the cashier for directions to "the place where barbecue is cooked over wood." He told me the way, and with other customers standing nearby warned that the quality of barbecue doesn't depend on either wood or gas, but on the type of sauce.

Walking out on another spirited debate, I headed for the outskirts of town. Here I found the Skylight Inn, a small, concrete-block building with a cola sign in front and a large gravel parking lot. Inside, Walter "Pete" Jones, owner and cook, welcomed me as if I had reached the final destination of a pilgrimage.

"You've come to the right place," he said. "You don't need to look any farther." Pete reached into a box and, with a smile on his broad face, presented me a white T-shirt. On its front, inside an outline of North Carolina, was "AYDEN, BAR-B-Q CAPITAL OF THE WORLD." On the back, the Pete Jones manifesto: "THE WOOD MAKES IT BAR-B-Q."

"If it's true barbecue, you don't need sauce," Pete said definitively as he leaned over the counter. "If you cook with gas, you have to add sauce. But if you cook with wood, you have the true barbecue flavor. You don't need anything else but vinegar and salt."

Pete uses oak. The ideal flavor, he said, comes from a mixture of 15 percent hickory and 85 percent oak, but hickory is scarce. In his cookroom across the parking lot, Pete burns the wood in a large fireplace, transferring the hot embers by shovel to homemade pits made of concrete and tin. He starts the fire at three in the morning and stokes it every thirty minutes. The meat is done by his 11 a.m. opening time. "Look at my arm," he said, holding out a thick red forearm. "It's cooked. That's from all the times I've held it over the fire." Pete began cooking barbecue with wood at age seven under the tutelage of his uncle; he has run his own business since 1940. "My great-great-granddaddy 150 years ago in Ayden was, I figure, the first person to sell barbecue to the public in Pitt County, and maybe all of North Carolina," Pete said. He sees himself now as the steward of a noble family tradition, staying with the "correct way" and resisting temptations to switch to the more economical and efficient gas pits.

To prove that wood is best, Pete arranged a taste test at his counter. He brought me a plate of his wood-cooked pork—chopped by hand with a cleaver—and a plate of a rival's gas-cooked meat, throwing in a soda, a slab of corn bread, and a dish of coleslaw that his wife had made in the back kitchen.

There was no contest. The crisp, smoky flavor of Pete's barbecue made it clearly superior to the other, which struck me as bland even when dressed with hot sauce. I asked other customers for their thoughts about the fare at the Skylight Inn. They responded as if they were auditioning for Skylight Inn commercials. They described the oak smoke as if it were a perfume, a back roads frankincense. Pete never stopped grinning as I cleaned off my plate.

So I called off my search, took the T-shirt, as well as a plate of pork to go, and—before the screen door slammed—promised Pete to spread the word about the true barbecue.

The Deep South, textbooks say, begins at the border of South Carolina. It had begun for me in Delaplane, Virginia, sixty miles from Washington, D.C. That's where I began hearing talk of the Confederacy, which to my northern ears sounded strangely exotic. In the Delaplane Store, operated by Louie "Teenie" Leas, the great-granddaughter of the man for whom Delaplane was named, a customer scolded me for not knowing the names of Confederate officers. A 73-year-old man across the road proudly showed me a pair of brass stirrups once owned by a Confederate cavalryman. Near Woodland, North Carolina, a tale-telling lawyer named William Burgwyn, whose great-uncle had died in the Battle of Gettysburg, took me to an abandoned country store full of dusty artifacts. There he dropped a nickel into a 1907 nickelodeon just so I could listen to "Dixie" and gaze upon a portrait of Gen. Robert E. Lee at the same time.

Thoughts of the Confederacy and the Union were especially in my mind by the time I reached South Carolina. I carried in my van a book published in 1857, *The Carolina Tribute to Calhoun*. A faint inscription on a front leaf made this volume about South Carolina statesman John C. Calhoun unusually evocative. It read: "This Book was captured from the Library of Benj. F. Dunkin at his private residence 'Midway,' Waccamaw River, S.C., as a trophy, Feby. 28th, 1865. Andw. Harman U.S.S. Mingoe." The book was Union booty from the Civil War. My mission—as I fancied it—was to find Midway, if it still existed, and return the volume to its rightful place.

The Waccamaw, I saw on the map, is one of several tidal rivers that drain what is known as the Low Country of South Carolina, near the coastal city of Georgetown. When I arrived there, sixty miles north of Charleston, I stopped at the local museum and discovered that Midway was the name of a rice plantation. In the first half of the 19th century, the Georgetown District, with its fertile marshland, ranked as the nation's principal rice-growing region. Some 200 plantations operated along the rivers, and the owners lived like kings.

At the city library I learned that Benjamin Faneuil Dunkin (1792-1874) had come to Charleston as a young tutor from Harvard. He stayed to become a distinguished lawyer, legislator, member of the secessionist movement, and chief justice of South Carolina—as well as absentee landlord of Midway. Additional reading revealed that the U.S.S. *Mingoe* had sailed into Winyah Bay on February 23, 1865, as part of a Union force that captured Georgetown less than two months before the Civil War ended.

Armed with this information, I set out to find the site of Midway. I followed dirt roads, studied maps, and talked with shopkeepers in the area north of Georgetown, near Pawleys Island, where the Waccamaw

Hughesville, Maryland   Rich and powerful aroma of cured tobacco hangs heavy
in the Farmers' Warehouse as buyers inspect last year's crop. To an auctioneer's chant—so rapid

that it remains unintelligible to an outsider—representatives of tobacco firms evaluate the quality of the leaf, make their bids, and buy at the rate of one basket every ten seconds.

North Carolina Tidewater

Lifting the tip of his fly rod, Herbert Jenkins of Aulander plays a fish toward his boat. His partner, Henry Rawls, meanwhile engages in the less spectacular—but far more common— aspects of the sport: sitting, watching the line, and listening to the rustle of the breeze through the leaves and to the lap of water against the skiff. At left, Rawls ties on a new leader. His tackle box holds a varied menu, and a tranquil afternoon promises time to try lure after lure.

plantations were located. After several hours, however, I had come up with nothing but dead ends. A downpour began, intensifying my discouragement. I was ready to abandon my search when luck stepped in. Stopping at an old frame rectory undergoing renovation, I had sprinted to the porch, where I met a carpenter who introduced himself simply as Blondell. He looked at the curious note in my book, puzzled over it a few seconds, and then said that he had once worked with a young black man named Benjamin Dunkin. Dunkin had mentioned, Blondell thought, that his ancestors had worked as slaves at Midway and had doubtless taken their master's name upon being freed. Blondell also told me that he thought Midway was now owned by one A. H. "Doc" Lachicotte.

Unfortunately, I was never able to locate Benjamin Dunkin, the black worker, but in the small resort village of Pawleys Island I did find Doc Lachicotte, a middle-aged entrepreneur who is a partner in a real estate firm. Sitting with his legs propped on his desk, dressed in loose khaki trousers and a white, short-sleeved shirt, chewing tobacco and speaking in a mumbled southern drawl, Doc confirmed that he indeed owned Midway. He and his partners had bought it and an adjacent plantation, True Blue, in 1971. The Lachicottes arrived in the Waccamaw River region in 1857, Doc told me, when his great-grandfather, Philip Rossignol Lachicotte, was hired to operate the rice mill at Brookgreen Plantation. By 1871 Philip Lachicotte had saved enough money to buy Waverly, a plantation the family still owns. The Lachicotte name remains prominent largely because of Doc, who, in addition to selling plantation lots, owns the popular Hammock Shop. No direct descendants of Benjamin F. Dunkin, the landowner, remain in the Georgetown area, Doc said. But if I wanted to see Midway, he would gladly show it to me. In the meantime, he urged me to take a look at what remained of some of the other Waccamaw plantations. Though most of the original mansions have burned or fallen down, and much of the land has been converted into subdivisions or farms, a few estates, such as Arcadia, recall the days of glory.

One afternoon Lucille Pate, owner of Arcadia and descendant of the railroad and shipping magnate Cornelius Vanderbilt, guided me around her expansive grounds, which back on the Atlantic Ocean and front on the Waccamaw River. We passed stables, a duck pond, a terraced garden leading to the river, a swimming pool, a tennis court, a bowling alley, a guesthouse, and a slave chapel still used on Sundays by local blacks. Deer and wild pigs live in the woods, Mrs. Pate told me. The plantation even maintains a game warden to prevent poaching. It was Mrs. Pate's great-grandfather, Capt. Isaac Emerson, developer of Bromo Seltzer, who furnished the grounds. One of the many wealthy Easterners who descended on the Low Country in the first third of the century, Emerson purchased six plantations between the years 1906 and 1925, and called his new holding Arcadia. He used the property as a hunting preserve before willing it in 1931 to his grandson, George Vanderbilt, who in turn left it to his only child, Lucille. She moved in full time in 1962.

"When Captain Emerson came, this house was in an extremely neglected state," said Mrs. Pate, who lives in the plantation house with her husband, Wallace, and their two young children. "He did extensive restoration, added two wings, and continued all the while to add to his holdings until, at the time of his death, he owned about 11,000 acres." The house, completed in 1794 and mentioned in the National Register of Historic Places as Prospect Hill, is a handsome white antebellum structure with bold pillars and spacious porches. The rice fields in the front are long overgrown, the province now of ducks, frogs, and snakes. Even so, Arcadia can make a visitor lose track of the century.

A wealthy Yankee named Archer M. Huntington, heir to a railroad fortune, visited the area north of Arcadia in 1930 and, taken with the beauty of the natural setting, bought four plantations. He named his estate Brookgreen Gardens. Here he and his wife, sculptor Anna Hyatt Huntington, created a magnificent formal garden, which they filled with sculptures.

"This was the first sculpture garden in the country. All others were

"I was born in the house my mother was born in," says William Hyslop Sumner Burgwyn, Jr., a North Carolina district attorney in Woodland. His forebears, who settled near here in the 1600s, include a great-uncle who died in the Civil War and a father who sat as a superior court judge until age 85.

copied from it," director Gurdon Tarbox, Jr., told me. "We have 410 different works from 183 artists, every one of them American." All of the pieces, Gurdon said, represent nature in one form or another. Today Brookgreen Gardens is a nonprofit organization administered by a board of 12 trustees. In addition to buying and displaying sculpture, Brookgreen Gardens is a center for the study of southeastern flora and fauna. Some 1,600 plant species grow on its 9,000 acres of swamp and pine barrens. Sanctuaries have been established for otters, alligators, deer, and such birds as the ibis and the blue heron.

It is the sculpture, however, situated amid the live oaks, palmettos, and dogwoods, that distinguishes the place. A walk in this southern garden turns up forms as commonplace as a squirrel or a pig, or as curious as an anteater; as fierce as a polar bear, or as benign as a sea horse. There are centaurs, nymphs, and fauns. Ben Franklin stands across from Zeus. It is a peaceable kingdom.

Across the Waccamaw River from Brookgreen Gardens, reachable only by boat, is Sandy Island, a 12,000-acre wedge of land that once held nine rice plantations. Its current population is 150, all blacks, most of them descendants of slaves who toiled in the area's rice fields. They live on the site of Mount Arena plantation, some 300 acres of which were bought by a former slave named Philip Washington. Electricity came to this isolated island in 1965, followed by the telephone in 1972. A respected patriarch handles the island's legal and political dealings with the outside world.

Gurdon Tarbox carried me to Sandy Island one day in an outboard. The riverbanks smelled of honeysuckle, and alligators peered out of the water, vanishing with a splash when we passed. Except for chickens, the island appeared deserted. A few low frame houses were visible on a hill. "Most of the men on the island commute to the mainland," Gurdon said, "to work as bricklayers, electricians, or boat operators." Until 1930 the islanders lived meager existences growing rice, but Archer Huntington came along to hire and train them to build his Brookgreen Gardens, and, as a result, a skilled work force has grown up.

Gurdon led me up a sandy path to the home of Rebecca Washington, at 82 the oldest person on the island and the widow of a former patriarch, Prince Washington. We settled in rocking chairs on her screened front porch, a refuge from the freshly hatched mayflies. The thin, white-haired "Miss Becca" talked about adapting to island life. "I was raised in Georgetown, and when I was married in 1914 I didn't know I was coming on the island. One thing I had before that I didn't have here was lights. I was brought up with lights. But everything worked out pretty well. I don't like crowds, and the place suited me."

The old woman brought out a photograph of her husband throwing a switch on a pole, bringing electricity to Sandy Island. I asked Miss Becca what she thought about this progress. "The Lord gave me light. He gave me telephone," she answered.

Later that day, about an hour before dusk, Doc Lachicotte led me to Midway, the object of my Waccamaw search. In two days I had seen in the transformation of the old rice plantations something of a microcosm of the new South: the preservation of antebellum grandeur at Arcadia; flourishing culture at Brookgreen Gardens; advances in the standard of living for blacks at Mount Arena; and now at Midway the drive toward development and growth.

Of the 1,900 acres that Doc and his partners bought at Midway and True Blue plantations, 44 lots of three to six acres apiece were recently snapped up within hours of the posted sale time, primarily by local people. The rest of the property has been surveyed for larger lots, for which Doc is looking for buyers. "With big tracts we can control what's being done," said Doc, a man whose desire for profit is tempered by a conscience that urges him to preserve the historical uniqueness of the area. "I have mixed emotions about development," he confessed when we first met. "I will develop the land—I can't keep up with the taxes otherwise—but I intend to keep this a residential community.

South Carolina
Low Country

Lofty sweet gums frame Prospect Hill, a historic mansion at Arcadia Plantation owned by Mr. and Mrs. Wallace Pate (above). "The frenzied pace of metropolitan life hasn't reached here yet," says Mrs. Pate. "But there's social life if you want it, and we can attend cultural events in Charleston, Columbia, or Myrtle Beach." Another reminder of the Old South, the tombstone of house slave Saunders (right) molders amid loblolly pines and sweet gums at Laurel Hill Plantation, part of Brookgreen Gardens a few miles north of Arcadia Plantation.

Just family residences, no condominiums. I think we can control it."

Doc unlocked a chain gate at the head of an overgrown road, and we walked down an avenue of live oaks. The giant, curving boughs and the green moss that hung from them like bunting evoked an atmosphere of great luxury. Yet, at the end of the avenue, by a lovely camellia amid the magnolia trees, there appeared only a large emptiness, a cool green space where once a mansion had stood. It had burned down, but no one seemed to know when. Two outbuildings have survived at the fringe of the plot—a smokehouse and a laundry shed. I could hear Doc wrestling with himself. "Whatever we do here will have the flavor of the Old South," he was saying. "A doctor's wife is eager to build a house here. But I don't care if I get a million dollars for the deed, I won't let those buildings get torn down."

Frogs were singing shrilly in the overgrown rice fields as I stood in the middle of the shaded area. All the grandeur and industry, wealth and ambition, and finally the ruin and disintegration that I had imagined because of a few words penciled in the front of a book had come to a haunting, peaceful close in this space of grass. The old fortunes had

In the dooryard of her home, one of eleven provided rent-free to Arcadia Plantation employees, retired laundress Mary Jenkins visits with Susan "Pigeon" Small (holding cane) and with Susan's great-granddaughter, Patricia Harris. Across the Waccamaw River, the New Bethel Baptist Church (above) stands on Sandy Island, a community of 150 blacks founded by a freed slave a century ago. The congregation erected the structure in 1951.

been wiped away, and now new ones would take their place. I was lost in reverie when Doc called for me to leave.

The next day, on my way out of the Low Country, I stopped at Doc's office and gave him the book.

From the coast I swung west through South Carolina, picking up elevation as I rolled through red fields of the Piedmont Region, climbing until I stood in clouds at 4,784 feet on the road atop Brasstown Bald in the mountains of north Georgia. I spent several days in this splendid high country at the southern end of the Appalachian Mountains. I hiked through forests of tall fir trees where invariably a waterfall awaited me, and I traveled the twisting roads in search of a handmade quilt. (I eventually bought one in the "continuing chain" pattern at Allie Thomas's stand on the road to Morganton.)

I was squarely in the Bible belt, and while here I attended my first revival meeting. On a Saturday night in Blairsville, while teenagers' cars rumbled down the main street, I took a pew in the Blairsville Christian Center, an interdenominational body whose members believe their ministers can invoke miracles with their prayers. Inside the brightly lit church, Danny Dyer, a blind evangelist who refers to God as "Our Heavenly Daddy" and uses a 28-volume braille Bible, was delivering a spirited sermon. "People think you get high by shooting up heroin," the thin, reformed alcoholic cried to his congregation. "But if you mainline Christ it's not illegal. You're getting high on Christ. There aren't any headaches or hangovers. Can you say Amen?" The faithful murmured "Amen," lifting their arms toward the ceiling.

I could barely follow the torrent of words. Instead of arousing the congregation, as I had expected, the sermon seemed to soothe the listeners, as if hypnotizing them. I had anticipated a jeremiad, with lurid emphasis on sinning and suffering, but instead Preacher Dyer stressed rejoicing and deliverance. This positive tone, together with the high-spirited singing (the hymns sounded like country-and-western tunes in this mountain church), made the experience enjoyable.

At the end of the two-hour sermon, several members of the congregation approached the front of the hall and asked the preacher to pray for them. A man complained of bronchitis; a woman said she didn't want to be frightened by thunderstorms any more. After hearing their pleas, Danny Dyer laid his hands on each of their heads, spoke loudly in an unintelligible tongue, and pronounced deliverance for each of his people, "in the faith of Jesus Christ."

Leaving the mountains behind, I plunged southward. Pines hemmed the roads, and I imagined myself being swept down a corridor toward Florida. Spring had turned warm, warm enough that I craved a swim. The resorts along the coast of Florida's panhandle were overflowing with people when I arrived on a mid-May weekend; billboards demanded that I have fun. I found an uncluttered beach thirty miles west of Panama City where the Gulf of Mexico's salt water buoyed me like a cork, and children played endlessly in the waves, as preoccupied as kittens with a moving finger.

Refreshed, I proceeded north into Alabama, passing through rickety towns with unpainted general stores; "jook joints"—dance halls —that come alive on Saturday nights; clusters of aging wooden houses; and graveyards sprouting bouquets of plastic flowers. About noon one day I reached Uniontown, a tidy-looking place with a population of 2,133, of which slightly more than half are blacks. Located in Perry County in west-central Alabama, the town once stood in the heart of a cotton kingdom; now it is a soybean domain.

In 1972, a man named Andrew M. Hayden ran for mayor of Uniontown. His opponent was Thomas R. Long, mayor for the previous 16 years. When the ballots had been counted, Hayden had won by 183 votes—590 to 407—and in so doing became the first black mayor in the town's history. The upset victory also made Hayden one of the few blacks in the state to be chosen to govern a biracial town.

I met Mayor Hayden, 59, at his desk in the newly built brick municipal building. Behind his chair on the wall hung his portrait; it included the slogan "We Shall Overcome" and a muted sketch of civil rights leader Martin Luther King, Jr. Both King and Hayden, the sons of ministers, had worked to register black voters in Perry County in the early 1960s, when such an undertaking amounted to a courageous and radical act. (Selma, where King led his famous nonviolent protest march in 1965, lies thirty miles east of Uniontown.) I asked Mayor Hayden, a tall, serious man with hair graying at his temples, what had compelled him to challenge the entrenched white rule in Uniontown.

"I sat on the City Council and Housing Authority for seven years, and some things were not happening that I thought *could* happen. My running for mayor was not a race-motivated thing. It was just that the power structure wasn't as sensitive as it should have been to some basic needs. The sewer system covered only 30 percent of the town, the main white district. The streets and sidewalks and improvements were always done in the white community. I ran on the premise that I'd work for the whole community. There were poor whites who were also being neglected. The power structure was slanted to the elite—to the people who had, not to the people who had not."

Campaigning vigorously in both the white and black communities, Hayden collected 59 percent of the vote. He won reelection in 1976 with 85 percent of the vote, which he considered a mandate to continue his attempt to improve the quality of life in Uniontown. Tapping public-works money from federal agencies, Hayden put his idealism into action. Sewers were extended to virtually all the town, dirt streets were paved, dilapidated houses were torn down or refurbished, new houses went up. The administration arranged for new public facilities, such as tennis courts, and it built the new municipal building. Hayden instituted regular city council meetings with public hearings. He selected a city staff of blacks and whites. "These seven years have provided a good indication of whether or not a black can do the work," he told me, with obvious gratification.

On a drive through town, Hayden pointed out improvements: "That house never had a toilet before." "This street used to be a mud lane." "These houses, homes of white families, have been fixed up." "This is a new housing development." I was seeing a town that had been resurrected. Hayden said his newest priority was attracting industry. Unemployment was high—12½ percent—and many of the townspeople were on welfare. During my visit, Hayden was actively courting a garment factory and a chicken-processing plant, hoping to persuade them to move their firms to Uniontown.

Despite all his evident successes, Hayden stressed that he was not altogether satisfied. The black and white communities had not come together as closely as he had envisioned. He laid part of the blame on past officials who have stayed "aloof," who "have not chipped in to help govern the community." But Hayden stood by his belief that his actions had benefited the people, both whites and blacks. "If I run again, and I think I will, I'll run on the record of what I've done. All I can say is, these things have happened, and they never happened before."

The election of black mayor Andrew Hayden points toward a new day in the South. Yet many Southerners, especially members of established white families, sometimes look back fondly to the old days of the plantations, when good breeding, a handsome estate, and a busy social life could make a person forget common cares and everyday routines. This nostalgia works as if to deny the passage of time altogether, and creates a kind of dream world where graciousness and good times mix as naturally as bourbon and branch water. Nostalgia is a pervasive force in southern life, I learned. And sometimes, when it can combine with a touch of purpose—as during a debutante party in the Mississippi Delta—the fantasy of the Old South truly flowers.

I reached the flat, fertile delta in late May, rendezvousing with photographer Ira Block and researcher Kathie Teter. We had been

Blairsville, Georgia

Surrendering herself and her problems to the Lord, a worshiper receives a laying on of hands at the Sunday morning anointing service of the Blairsville Christian Center. "I cannot heal anyone or anything," says the Reverend Wofford Kelley, pastor of the church (left) since 1978. "I obey the word of God by laying hands on them and praying for them in the name of Jesus, and the Lord heals them." At right, a member of the congregation follows the injunction of I Timothy 2:8–"I will therefore that men pray every where, lifting up holy hands."

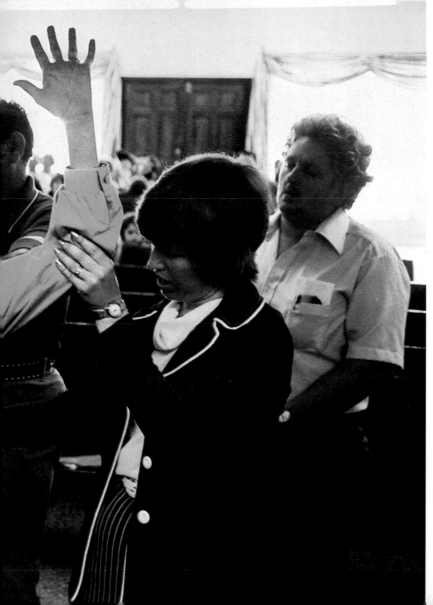

invited to a garden party held by the Southern Debutante Assembly at a plantation outside Greenwood. This would be the first social function of the debutante season, which runs until Christmas. Then, at the Gold and White Ball in Greenwood, 27 young women, all of well-known Mississippi families, would be presented to society.

The garden party—held so the debutantes could begin meeting one another—was scheduled for early evening, and by late afternoon a general feeling of glee had already spread among officials. The reason: The sky had cleared. For the past couple of months rain had drenched the delta. The cotton fields lay under puddles. Worst spring in memory, moaned the cotton farmers, who are known in the delta as planters. At four o'clock the leaden sky had begun to lighten, right on time for the area's most prestigious springtime social event. And delta families just love to be social, I was repeatedly told. "We'll drive a hundred miles to go to a cocktail party," the wife of a planter said, as the flush of an agreeable memory spread across her face.

The party took place at Nebo Plantation near Schlater, about 15 miles northwest of Greenwood. I asked Mrs. James Pierce Cole, Jr., whose family owns the manor house, where the name had come from. "Nebo is the name of the mountain Moses stood on to view the Promised Land," she replied. On the local promised land at that moment, the debutantes were making a final check of their appearance. They reminded me of swans as they glided across the lawn in their long dresses, stopping in groups under tall oaks where, with looks of languor and innocence, they posed for official photographs.

"We are honoring the ideal of southern womanhood," Mrs. William Hemingway Montjoy had exclaimed at a dinner the previous night. Mrs. Montjoy and the other officers—or doyennes—of the Southern Debutante Assembly speak proudly of most aspects of their society. They distinguish it from debutante organizations in many large southern cities that, in their judgment, have become "commercial." "Here, one is invited to become a debutante not merely because of an affluent family," said Mrs. John Thomas McMillan.

The criteria the Southern Debutante Assembly uses for selecting its young women remain vague, however. "It's just there, you can't analyze it," said one guest. Another joked: "You don't want them to be from a family of horse thieves." What is important, I gathered, is that the debutante hail from a respectable family that goes back several generations in the state.

Whatever their qualifications, the debutantes at Nebo Plantation appeared eager for the season to begin. Before the guests arrived, I made a practice run down the receiving line and talked with the debs. Many had grown up on plantations away from cities, and almost all were freshmen at southern colleges where they had joined sororities. Their bright, pretty faces made me think of cheerleaders. They held baskets of white daisies. Their manners were impeccable, and none of them seemed defensive about taking part in this exclusive ritual. Many said they accepted the debutante society's invitation out of a feeling of obligation to their families, but others admitted that the expectation of a year of parties, of traveling around the state, and of making new friends was also important.

"It's fun. There are all kinds of parties and dancing. I'm no fool." Dark-haired, dark-eyed Sarah Buford thus offered her reasons for making the debutante circuit. Sarah was *(Continued on page 88)*

Uniontown, Alabama
Andrew M. Hayden, first black mayor in the town's history, looks to the future confidently. First elected in 1972 by a margin of 183 votes, he won reelection four years later. "My running for mayor was not a race-motivated thing," he says. "I ran on the premise I'd work for the whole community."

Hale County, Alabama   Siren's howl pierces the soft southern night as state trooper John Christenberry pursues a speeder. At upper right, he fills out a summons, then props up a highly polished shoe as he places a call (above, left) about an accident he investigated earlier. Beside him in his car (right) sits a stuffed rabbit—a good-luck charm friends gave him after escaped convicts riddled his vehicle with *12* shotgun blasts; he walked away with only minor cuts. A ten-year veteran of the force, he says: "Seems like I have an ability for running up on very dangerous situations."

Nebo Plantation   Young women of the Southern Debutante Assembly receive delta plantation society at a May 31 garden party near Greenwood, Mississippi. The function initiates

the assembly's debutante season. Participants cherish such rituals, confident that they uphold honored traditions of the Old South—good manners, good breeding, and gracious living.

Last-minute adjustment of a hem occupies Louise Vaughan and Pi Dale (kneeling) on the grounds of Nebo Plantation (opposite). Whiling away the minutes before the first guests arrive at the garden party, author Tom O'Neill talks with several of the debutantes (below) as photographer Ira Block records the scene. At left, Sarah Buford, a student at Southern Methodist University in Dallas, holds the traditional basket of daisies. "It's fun," she says of participation in the debutante season. "There are all kinds of parties and dancing."

KATHLEEN F. TETER, NATIONAL GEOGRAPHIC STAFF

At the entrance to the Nebo Plantation manor house, Mississippi debutantes pose for their official portrait. The plantation's name derives from Mount Nebo, traditionally the place where Moses first viewed the Promised Land.

wearing an off-white, lace-edged gown. After the garden party, she said, she would return to Memphis, where she was participating in the Cotton Carnival. "I've worn a long dress every night since Saturday," she said gaily, on this Thursday evening. Like many of the debutantes, Sarah, of Glendora, insisted she is going to college—Southern Methodist University in Dallas—to prepare for a career. "Daddy said I should get a degree so I could do something if anything happened to my husband," she said. "So I'm studying biology. It's a security."

"Everyone has the impression that women from the South get married and sit at home," complained Patti Harbin, who grew up in Grenada, Mississippi, and is studying to be a dietitian at the University of Mississippi. "We're not all interested in that. We're liberated—just a little." She held her thumb and forefinger an inch apart. "Just enough to do *something* that is considered better than just sitting on the front porch. It's easier to have both a family and a career in the South. The pace is slower."

Semmes Evans, of Shuqualak, was enjoying the pageantry. "I think this is an honor," she said excitedly. "It's your time in the limelight. Everyone is staring at you. This kind of reverts back to the Old South. If I had my way, I'd have lived then. This is like being in a play."

The performance began at seven o'clock when the first of 700 guests arrived. The debutantes had taken their positions in six semi-circles on the lawn in front of the brick manor house. For the next two hours they welcomed society, which in this case consisted largely of the members of old delta families. To each guest the deb would state her name and the place where she grew up, and then, if necessary, engage in polite conversation about relatives and hometowns.

Young men, dressed in white dinner jackets, were sprinkled throughout the well-wishers. They belonged to a bachelor society known as the Cavaliers, hand-picked for the debutante season. The Southern Debutante Assembly's handbook described them as "high-type gentlemen for whom we make no apology when they are introduced to our debutantes."

On another part of the lawn, the pages to the debutantes—girls in the eighth grade—stood in a receiving line of their own. Music drifted from the porch, where two men were playing Broadway tunes on an accordion and a saxophone. Under a wisteria arbor, women in white dresses served punch and white wine.

Perhaps it was the wine (I think not), but as the evening wore on, and the hurricane lamps illuminated the garden, and young women stood serenely under 200-year-old trees offering gloved hands to chivalrous young men, I felt light-headed. I stepped to the porch and, while the curtain of warm darkness fell, believed for an instant that nothing existed beyond this group of people going through their elegant motions. The party had been a success. Time had scudded away like a sky full of clouds.

It's a 45-mile drive from the plantation garden at Schlater to an unpainted wooden house in Leland. James "Son" Thomas, a tall, spindly black man with a worn face, was sitting on a chair in his front room playing a slide guitar. His voice came sweet and plaintive:

> *I said beefsteak when I'm hungry, whiskey when I'm dry,*
> *Good-looking women while I'm living, heaven when I die.*
> *Going away to leave you. Worry you off my mind.*
> *Well, you keep me worried, bothered all the time.*
> *Some folks say them old worried, worried blues ain't bad.*
> *Well now, it's the worst old feelin' that I most ever had.*

Son Thomas was playing the blues, one counterpart in the delta of the dreamy gentility of plantation life. I had met Thomas, who is regarded as one of the best country bluesmen still in the delta, in a cafe across from the railroad tracks. In his aging station wagon we crossed the tracks to the black section of town. We hardly spoke. When we reached his place, Son Thomas pulled out an electric guitar, an acoustic guitar, and a battered Sears Roebuck amplifier. Sitting in front of the double bed that practically filled the hot, airless room, he played. The songs were by such delta blues kings as Robert Johnson and Sonny Boy Williamson. A couple of men from the neighborhood, hearing the guitar, stopped in to listen and sip whiskey. Son Thomas hunched over

Riot of kudzu smothers other vegetation beside a Mississippi road. Introduced from Japan and widely planted during the thirties for erosion control and soil enrichment, kudzu has since become a pest. Its vines can grow a foot a day.

the guitar and delivered music that at one instant was urgent and playful, like conversation in a bar, and in another moment was sad and soothing, like a far-off train whistle. After four songs, Son Thomas put down the guitar and began talking.

"Blues is a feeling," he said, chewing on a cold biscuit and a piece of fried pork. "I never had a religion, but I imagine religion feels sorta like the blues. It makes you feel good doing it."

The blues were nurtured in the Mississippi Delta, growing out of the work chants that black laborers sang while toiling in the cotton fields for white bosses. The music eventually evolved into a conscious outlet for the feelings of people in the black communities. "People had such hard times, with low pay, that everyone had the blues," explained Thomas, the son of a sharecropper. "People couldn't come out and speak to you like they wanted to. They had to sing to make them feel better."

Workers were constantly singing in the fields, Thomas said. "They might be plowing with a mule or driving a tractor way back in the fields by themselves. Some of them had songs with words like *Captain, Captain, why are you so mean?* They couldn't walk up to the overseer and say it, so they sang it." The source of the blues is fairly simple, Thomas said. "It is women and hard work and low pay—or what you-all call low income now."

Thomas began playing his uncle's guitar when he was a small boy, paying a dollar each time he used it. He memorized the music of early blues records he heard on his grandmother's gramophone in Eden, and he would sneak into roadhouses to hear bottleneck guitarists like Elmore James. Once he could handle a guitar, Thomas began performing at jook joints and house parties, where, he said, "someone was always pulling a gun or a knife." During the day he dug graves.

Thomas was "discovered" in 1967 by William Ferris, at that time a graduate student in folklore at the University of Pennsylvania. Ferris had been searching the delta for rural musicians. Thomas had never

traveled outside the delta, but with the help of Ferris he began performing at universities, clubs, and folk-life festivals in places such as
Delaware, Maine, and Washington, D.C.—locations he speaks of as if
they were foreign countries. Still, though he has recorded two albums,
Thomas remains largely unknown outside the delta. When his back
began to hurt, he quit digging graves and went to work for a furniture
store. He doesn't work steadily now, but waits patiently for letters or
phone calls inviting him to play.

During the afternoon we spent together, Thomas would, in
moments of silence, pick up his guitar and fool with a song as idly as if
he were whittling. When he talked about music, he would recite a blues
verse to punctuate his point, like a preacher quoting Scripture. I asked
him how his style of blues differed from that of his predecessors. "Most
times when you see me singing the blues, I got my mind on money. I'll
think about women later. Long time ago you didn't have to have much
money. That's why they sang about women. Now you need money to
run the show." With that he fixed me in the eye and said:

> *If you go to Vicksburg and start calling my name,*
> *The women will start falling like showers of rain.*
> *Cows and hogs all need oats and hay.*
> *The women getting glad because it my payday.*

Late in the afternoon, Thomas's teenage son, Raymond, visited the
house. He picked up a guitar and spun some simple blues licks.
Thomas had recently given Raymond a guitar and had been teaching
him the blues. However, he told me, he suspects that Raymond is more
interested in disco, that omnipresent spin-off of soul music. After a
time, Raymond put down the guitar, and then it was only Son Thomas
playing. He did his talking with music, as he bent over his instru-
ment—his long fingers snaking down its neck, his voice high and
intense. As Son Thomas lost himself in the tune, a grin spread across
Raymond's face, as if in amazement at his father's unabashed emotion.
Son Thomas was playing the blues.

Ever since I was a child I've had difficulty accepting the fact that
the dividing line between spring and summer has to do with
the position of the sun on a particular day in June. It seems too
precise and immutable an indicator for the change of a season. My
homespun method often relied on temperature: When did the lasting
onslaught of warm weather arrive, forcing people to their fans and
short sleeves? A deep-fry heat had certainly begun to settle in as I
explored the South, venturing north as far as Memphis and south to
Jackson, Mississippi. As I drove through Louisiana to Texas, relief
would come sporadically with sudden squalls that dropped dense cur-
tains of rain. Within minutes of these cooling showers, however, the air
would thicken, becoming hotter and muggier than before.

My second determinant of spring's end was simpler: Spring ended
on the last day of school. Thus I found myself in late May attending a
high school graduation ceremony in the east Texas town of Douglass,
population 75.

Inside the auditorium of Douglass Independent School, the graduating class of 1979 occupied one and a half rows of chairs. They
numbered nine. This class is considered large; the previous year five
seniors graduated. The total number in the high school, which serves

Leland, Mississippi   *His guitar within reach, blues musician James "Son" Thomas sips beer beneath an earlier portrait in the Main Street Cafe. He has appeared on the "Today" show, recorded two albums, and served several terms as artist-in-residence at Yale University.*

western Nacogdoches County, is 31. This results in a certain amount of privilege. All 14 boys made the basketball team. Most of the seniors served on the staff of *Chinquapin*, the school's folklore journal.

Despite the small graduating class, the auditorium was packed with parents, brothers and sisters, and friends. On the stage sat a man with glasses and neatly slicked hair, wearing a suit. He was James H. Milstead, the school's superintendent. Mr. Milstead is a disciplinarian. He believes in the virtue of corporal punishment—paddling the students for behavioral and scholastic shortcomings. "Wood has been put on every offender, and few finish school without the 'board of education,'" he said forthrightly. Hair must be neat, smoking is prohibited, and students may not drive their cars during school hours.

The seniors looked a bit uncomfortable in their purple robes and mortarboards, with white tassels tickling their ears. They claimed they appreciated the discipline, but also assured me that they were, for better or worse, typical students, citing smoke bombs exploding in lavatories and a motorcycle being driven through the school halls. The five boys and four girls in the class also said they enjoyed the intimacy of a small school where they knew everybody. A few planned to enroll in a junior college in the area. The thought of attending a larger school, however, made them nervous.

The microphone squeaked as redheaded Ritchey Butler delivered the class history. Ritchey, in good voice, mentioned the moon landing, the end of the Vietnam War, and the Israeli-Egyptian peace treaty as milestones of his classmates' last 12 years. Valedictorian Vickie Perkins, also redheaded, confidently told her classmates not to expect to follow "a yellow brick road," but to make sure that whatever their path, "it leads to God."

During the speeches, a loud, furious storm was raging outside; lightning lit up the night and thunder interrupted the speakers. As the heavens raged, the next speaker stepped to the podium to deliver the commencement address. He was a public relations official with Texas Power and Light who had grown up in the area. Just as he finished his introductory jokes and began moving into his speech, a cannonade of thunder exploded outside, and the lights went out. The auditorium lay in darkness. Nobody tittered or spoke. When the lights suddenly flickered back on, the Texas Power and Light representative soberly resumed his remarks on dedication and determination and hard work as if nothing unrehearsed had happened.

With the speeches ended and the rain beating a dramatic tattoo on the roof, the nine seniors marched across the stage to accept their diplomas from principal Robert Baker. Cameras clicked and whirred like cicadas as each student went through the graduation choreography: taking a diploma, shaking the principal's hand, walking stiffly to the middle of the stage, and, with a dedicated and determined look, flipping the tassel from the left side of the cap to the right. Smile. Click. Whirrr. Spring had ended.

The *Class* of 1979

Clockwise, from above:
**BRENDA DECKARD
DEBBIE CARROLL
PHYLLIS HAYTER
JIM WHITAKER, JR.
STEVEN MILSTEAD**

Last rites of spring: Joey Tarrant, one of the nine 1979 graduates of Douglass Independent School in Texas, flips the tassel of his mortarboard to the right after receiving his diploma from school principal Robert Baker. That ritual, as any high school senior will attest, signifies more than any other that summer has finally arrived.

Clockwise,
from above:

RITCHEY BUTLER
JOEY TARRANT
VICKIE PERKINS
JACK ALLEN

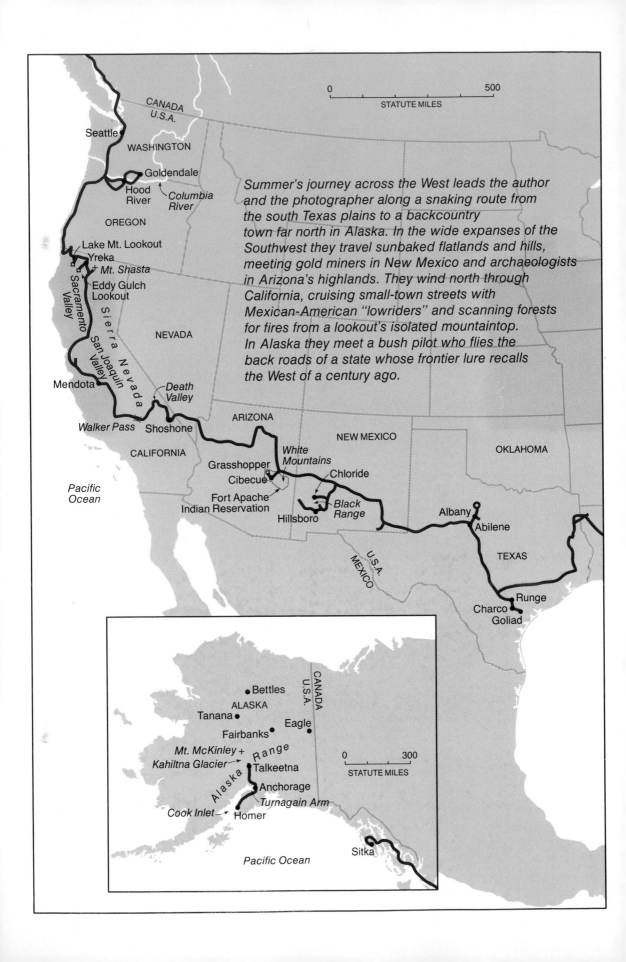

Summer's journey across the West leads the author and the photographer along a snaking route from the south Texas plains to a backcountry town far north in Alaska. In the wide expanses of the Southwest they travel sunbaked flatlands and hills, meeting gold miners in New Mexico and archaeologists in Arizona's highlands. They wind north through California, cruising small-town streets with Mexican-American "lowriders" and scanning forests for fires from a lookout's isolated mountaintop. In Alaska they meet a bush pilot who flies the back roads of a state whose frontier lure recalls the West of a century ago.

CANADA
U.S.A.

Seattle

WASHINGTON

Goldendale
Hood River
Columbia River

OREGON

Lake Mt. Lookout
Yreka
+ Mt. Shasta
Eddy Gulch Lookout

Sacramento Valley

Sierra Nevada

San Joaquin Valley

NEVADA

Mendota

Death Valley

Walker Pass   Shoshone

ARIZONA

CALIFORNIA

Pacific Ocean

White Mountains

Grasshopper
Cibecue

Fort Apache Indian Reservation

Hillsboro

Chloride

Black Range

NEW MEXICO

OKLAHOMA

Albany
Abilene

TEXAS

MEXICO
U.S.A.

Runge
Charco
Goliad

0   500
STATUTE MILES

Bettles

ALASKA

Tanana

Eagle

Fairbanks

CANADA
U.S.A.

Mt. McKinley +
Kahiltna Glacier

Alaska Range

Talkeetna

Anchorage
Turnagain Arm

Cook Inlet

Homer

Sitka

Pacific Ocean

0   300
STATUTE MILES

Summer

IT HAD BEEN one of those hot south Texas days. The green of the trees was the green of vegetables boiled too long. Harsh sunlight made the landscape look stark and deserted. Drowsiness affected us like a drug.

Walter Scott, cattle rancher from Goliad, sat motionless inside the bunkhouse. His wide-brimmed hat was pulled over his eyes; the pain of a headache tugged at the corners of his mouth.

Walter, a graduate of Baylor University in Waco, is a former president of the Texas Longhorn Breeders Association of America and a director of the Texas and Southwestern Cattle Raisers Association. For the past 15 years, he has played an important role in the preservation of the Texas longhorn breed.

According to western movies and novels—those purveyors of Texas mythology—a cattle rancher earns a headache from a bout of drinking, or in a barroom brawl, or from being thrown from a horse. Walter Scott scoffs at such an image of western life. If he would talk now, Walter would probably describe the realistic, even prosaic, cause of his headache: A roundup had not gone smoothly. Dealing with a bunch of Texas longhorns, four children, and two cowhands, all under a brain-baking sun, had left him feeling tired and worn.

Finally, Walter broke his silence and began to speak dreamily: "My idea of a really fine vacation would be to take my two best mares, my number one saddle and my number two saddle, a bridle and a bedroll, and go to work with a crew of experienced cowmen and trained hands."

Despite myself, I couldn't help thinking that Walter had just delivered a line from a Hollywood movie. It must be tough for cattlemen, especially self-described pragmatists like Walter, to wean themselves from the mythology—to devote time and money, as Walter is doing, to buying a new bulldozer for clearing pastures, to building additional fences for rotational grazing, to constructing ponds for storing water. Here is a traditional, hard-bitten cowman trying to ride with the long arm of progress.

At the end of the day, sipping bourbon, with his boots propped on a table, Walter said, "A good cowhand is a man on a horse who's at the right place at the right time. He has to know enough 'bovine psychology' to be able to anticipate what cows are going to do." He flicked a sharp look at me, as if daring me to find such a man.

Driving across Texas in June, I had succumbed to the mystique of the state. True, I could have found a ranch in Montana or Wyoming, where cowboys contend with terrain and climate as demanding as any in Texas. Yet Texas is a special case. Because of its history as the birthplace of the American range-cattle industry and the starting point of those storied trail drives, I had come to believe that it had been created for no other purpose than to hold herds of cattle watched over by men on horseback. (Continued on page 104)

South Texas *Rangeland as enduring as its cowboy lore feeds longhorn herds and a cattleman's dreams. Astride a gray mare, rancher Walter Scott leads a roundup near Runge.*

Descended from cattle introduced by early Spaniards, Texas longhorns had all but vanished by the 1920s; Walter Scott works to revive the hardy strain—symbol of an untamed West.

*G*alloping hooves mark the rhythm of roundup at Walter Scott's Copa de Vino ranch as Scott and his son Eric corral a longhorn. They ride two of Scott's forty registered quarter horses, a quick and versatile breed. Scott relies on his family's skills to help manage his herd. His youngest child, Stephanie, 12 (left), watches as three of her four brothers wrestle a heifer to the ground (right); Anthony and Eric Scott hold rear and front legs; cowhand Roy Holdcroft straddles the calf; and friend Robert Edison turns the animal's head as Michael Scott attaches a numbered tag to its ear.

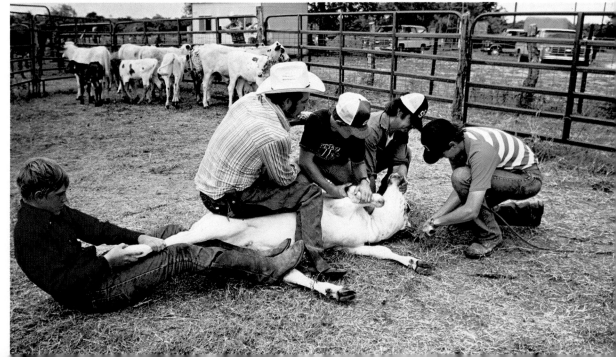

*C*old beer and cattle talk relax the patrons of Ann's Place in Runge. Walter Scott, his legs outstretched, speaks with farmer "Judge" Linhart. Cowhands Roy Holdcroft and Jerry Johnson share the table, and local merchant Hill Garza, seated at right, joins them after a day of roundup. "In the noonday heat of south Texas, the shade the bars offered became a palpable pleasure," says the author. Facing a cluster of empty Lone Star beer bottles, Jerry Johnson (above) smiles and orders one more round.

Afternoon stillness settles like dust on an abandoned corner of the Goliad town square. Third oldest municipality in Texas, Goliad once saw action in the Texas Revolution; empty streets now reflect more peaceful times.

So I had stopped in south Texas at Walter Scott's ranch, where the entrance sign reads *Copa de Vino,* Spanish for "wineglass." The operation carries about 300 registered and branded Texas longhorns on well over a thousand acres of land. It is divided into three pastures stretching between the little towns of Runge and Goliad.

The world likes to believe the flavorful stories about Texans, yet after only a few days on the ranch I realized that the vivid, time-forged definitions of cowboy and cattleman were breaking down—changing in response to new conditions, leaving the myths to dissolve like images on a screen.

"I have to be a mechanic, plumber, engineer, financier, and banker—and that's just part of it," explained Walter, an intense, reflective, sometimes irascible man who is struggling to come to terms with these multiple roles. "The day of the old cowboy is dead," he continued. "Time was, the cowboy spent all day with the cows and could fairly accurately tell how a cow was doing. Now most cowboys have little understanding of the proper handling of livestock—no 'cow sense.' Besides, cowboys are in rodeos. Cow*men* run ranches."

The roundup that day had begun in midmorning in a pasture near Charco. Walter wanted to gather this herd to match mothers with calves born during the winter and to pull some stock to sell. To help, there were the two hands and four of Walter's five children—Michael, 17, Eric, 15, Anthony, 14, and his one daughter, Stephanie, 12. Richard, 16,

Off the crew rode into a stand of mesquite. On a larger ranch, one of those gigantic cattle spreads with hundreds of thousands of acres, a roundup might take more than a week to complete. Walter intended to finish his work at Charco in just one day.

Soon after the riders disappeared, I heard the crack of bullwhips and the hollering of the riders. Within minutes, bellowing Texas longhorns were racing out of the brush as if it were on fire. Unfortunately, Walter's saddle cinch broke, and he was unable to cut off the herd and steer the animals into the pens. The cattle scattered.

After making repairs, Walter gathered up his crew, and they entered the brush again. This time they successfully bottled up the cattle and herded them into the pens. The only hitch came when a brown-and-white calf broke from the herd and tore for freedom. It required four riders, along with people afoot yelling and waving hats, to chase it into confinement.

Inside a pen, Walter, chewing on a cigar and holding a bullwhip, waited until the cattle had settled down. Then the hands cut the calves from the herd and grappled them, one at a time, to the ground. They notched the calves' ears in the ranch's registered pattern and attached numbered ear tags. The calves are branded with the outline of a wineglass in the fall when they are weaned.

Meanwhile, Walter's wife was keeping careful records of the tag number, sex, and markings of each calf. "It's a family operation," says Walter. So Mary Elizabeth not only manages the house, but also keeps the account books and cattle records of the ranch, and still finds time to serve on the school board and to do church work.

Needless to say, penning cattle is not always an easy operation. In the heat, all the riders lost their tempers at one time or another.

When the cattle that were not to be sold had been released into the pasture and the horses loaded onto a trailer, we drove the 18 miles back to the ranch house. Before dinner, Walter, his headache gone, stepped into his office to tend to paperwork. He settled behind a large desk, put on a pair of reading glasses, and began shuffling through papers. He had looked more at ease chasing cattle on his horse. The office work, however, is vital to the success of an operation, Walter admits.

"We can't be ranchers any more," he said ruefully. "We're stock farmers. This means I should devote 90 percent of my time to this desk—reading books on artificial insemination and embryo transplant, on legislation affecting land development, on advertising and animal science." His voice became determined. "This is my livelihood—not a hobby. I've got to keep abreast of changes and developments in the industry if I expect to remain a success."

It might seem ironic that Walter Scott, while accommodating himself to the role of a modern businessman, is raising an old-fashioned breed of cattle—the Texas longhorn. Almost extinct by the 1920s, the Texas longhorn has revived largely because of efforts of men like Walter who think its genetic qualities—hardiness, ease of calving, resistance to disease—should be bred back into cattle.

Walter admits that he was born a hundred years too late. "I always wanted to be a rancher, never wanted to be a farmer and own a tractor," Walter said at his desk as the sky darkened outside. "I wanted thousands of acres and ten good men riding the best horses. But that's a

Albany, Texas   A dream come true brings a smile to Morris Tidmore's face as he stands proudly beside his backyard oil well. "Always wanted me some oil, some of my own," recalls the retired oil worker. In 1943 he purchased land for his home on a hunch that black gold lay underfoot; when he drilled in 1960, it paid off—and the oil still flows.

dream. How's a man going to put it together? It's impossible, unless you have another source of income." He shook his head slowly, as if to dispel the dreams that would not leave him alone. With a resolute look, he returned to his papers.

A cattleman's dream may require thousands of acres, as does Walter's, but in the small Texas town of 'Albany, 35 miles northeast of Abilene, the dream needed only a backyard. I drove into Albany, population 1,978, in early July and stopped in front of a modest one-story house set in a residential neighborhood. Seventy-two-year-old Morris Tidmore, a large, easygoing Texan with a comfortable paunch beneath his khaki work clothes, showed me around his yard. I saw a wishing well, a goldfish pond, a vegetable garden, a small corral for the saddle horse, a row of peach trees, an oil well. An oil well?

Marked by a pumping unit known as a "nodding donkey," the well sits in the middle of the neat garden as if it were a part of the landscaping. It doesn't belong to an oil firm, a land company, or the state or federal government. It is Morris Tidmore's own: He doesn't share the royalties with anyone.

His story, told in a matter-of-fact drawl, begins in 1923 when he was an ambitious teenager. "I was raised on a little old sandy farm in east Texas, and at that time you couldn't make a living to save your neck. I was about 16 when I started hunting for a job in an oil field. Heard the work was pretty good. Well, I started down at Moran, about 15 miles south of here. My first job was hauling water in a Model T Ford truck. I had hauled water about a week when the driller's helper got hurt, and the head driller asked me if I wanted the job. It paid fifty cents an hour. It beat farming."

Morris thus began his career in the oil fields. Whenever a new discovery was announced, off he went, living in tents in the boomtowns of Louisiana, Texas, Oklahoma, New Mexico, and Arizona. He learned most of the jobs associated with drilling oil, losing a thumb in the process, but gaining in the meantime a vision. "I thought I'd get rich someday. Always wanted me some oil, some of my own. I never had any money, but I made up my mind while I was drilling big wells for other people, making them rich, I made up my mind I'd get me some oil before I died."

While working on the rigs, Morris began to dabble in oil exploration in the Albany area, but all the wells he invested in came up dry. Throughout this frustrating period, Morris never forgot his hole card—his own backyard. In 1943 he built a house in Albany, specifically picking the land because of a hunch that oil lay beneath it. The yard stayed untried until 1960, when he had finally saved enough money— about $1,500—to attempt his first solo exploration. "I leased a rig—an old spudder—and bought casing and cement, and didn't have a dollar left. I had to buy groceries on credit."

For six weeks Morris drilled, watching a large steel bit gouge a hole in the ground. When he passed the 600-foot mark near the end of the year, he was ready to quit, having exhausted his money. But fortune finally intervened. On Christmas Day—"I'm telling the truth," he says with a laugh—oil began to spit out of the ground, gloriously growing into a flow. Morris ran around his backyard shouting and screaming. At last he had some oil of his own.

Morris figures that since 1960 he's pumped 12,000 barrels of oil from the 691-foot-deep well. In the beginning, it produced a hundred

Chloride, New Mexico *Jagged hills of the Black Range rise above the weathered buildings of Chloride, a silver-mining town of the 1880s in the southwestern corner of*

the state. Now only a handful of families and old-timers live here. Scores of ghost towns sprinkle quiet pockets of the Southwest, monuments to the rollicking boom-and-bust days.

*O*ne man's ghost town is another man's home: Raymond Schmidt (opposite) prepares to mount his Honda by his house in Chloride, where he has lived for most of his 83 years. A former miner and fire lookout, Schmidt enjoys the peaceful isolation of Chloride, where grasses and blossoms encroach on crumbling buildings such as the old Sierra County Bank (left). The vagaries of weather here can alter plans: A flash flood (below), a common occurrence during heavy summer rains, washes out a stretch of State 52 near Chloride.

barrels a day, and within three months Morris was making pure profit. A well is like a person, however, Morris reflectively points out: Each day it gets used up just a little more. The well is presently good for only half a barrel a day. Morris has considered capping it, but his wife wants it to stay in operation. "It is a visible property asset," she says.

That Christmas Day did not, of course, halt Morris's obsession with oil. In his free time away from his heavy-construction business, he continued drilling within the township limits—on his wife's grandparents' property, on land next to his church, in a neighbor's yard. "Every time I'd get enough money, I'd drill another. That's the fever." Morris estimates that he's drilled ten dry wells for every successful one, and has ended up with four producing wells in Albany. They are called strippers, wells that produce less than ten barrels a day. Strippers account for about 70 percent of the nation's wells and provide some 15 percent of the domestic crude oil supply.

In 1971, an electrocardiogram revealed heart trouble, and Morris retired from business. But his interest in oil would not go away. Borrowing money, he leased forty stripper wells in the vicinity of Moran, only a few miles from where fifty years earlier he had taken his first job in an oil field. His timing was perfect. In 1973, before the Arabian oil-producing countries imposed an embargo on oil exports and began raising prices, Morris was selling his oil for $3.50 a barrel. In 1979, he was receiving $38.50 a barrel. For the first time in his life, newly retired Morris Tidmore was making a lot of money from oil.

"When I bought the leases, I was only looking for something to do," he says with convincing ingenuousness. "I would have been content just to make expenses. People said I was smart. No, it was nothing but luck," Morris laughs. "Some fellow asked me what I thought of the Arabs, and I said, 'I love 'em.' Wouldn't you?"

Most mornings, before he gets tired, Morris steps into a new

Hillsboro, New Mexico

Hillsboro General Store holds something for everyone: pots for the housewife, pans for the miner, food for tourists, feed for livestock, relics, a copying machine, and—always— conversation for the road-worn traveler. "While on the back roads," says the author, "I learned that the local bars and the country stores are the real sources of news and information. To find out what was going on in a community, I'd stop first at a general store, not at a town hall." Though it now has only about 150 residents, Hillsboro once lay at the heart of a rich and populous gold-mining district; the general store still supplies the occasional prospector who hopes to find an untapped vein.

*F*resh stirrings of gold fever lure miners to the hills of New Mexico in search of deposits overlooked by prospectors a century ago. At his Dutch Gulch claim east of Hillsboro, Dave McCravey (left) scoops up gold-bearing gravel deposits—or placers. After washing the earth through a sluice box (top), he pans out tiny flecks of "the yeller" (above) that earlier miners once found in nuggets and veins.

pickup and, like a benign landlord, drives into the country to check his wells. Often he simply makes sure the pumping units are working with metronomic regularity. Other times he dips a gauge into the thick blackness of the storage tanks to determine how much oil a well is producing in a day.

Morris says he is a contented man, that he has all he needs. Of his 44 wells, only 11 are working, averaging a total of twenty barrels a day. He's leaving the rest underground for his children and grandchildren. Yet, as we stood in the backyard watching the pump nod at us, Morris confessed with a grin that he is looking at just one more lease west of town. And speaking of town, the best remaining site for oil in Albany is right in the middle of the high school football field, Morris contends. "I'd have oil there if they'd let me have it." I believe him.

Beyond Albany stretch the long, empty distances of the West.

"This is our drive-in movie," says Dave McCravey, as he and watchman Pat O'Brack prop up their feet to watch a television show framed in McCravey's mobile home window. Along the horizon, dusk darkens the slopes of nearby Animas Peak. With chilled beer and cool night air for refreshment, the two men enjoy an evening's entertainment, back roads style.

Occasionally a pickup would fill my rearview mirror and gun around me, but mostly I was alone on the road, contemplating the distant high ground that floated in the heat like a hazy cloud. The tang of sagebrush scented the air, and the sun burned in the sky like a branding iron. In New Mexico, the town markers didn't list population; instead, they gave the elevation, often a larger number. I passed through several crossroads towns; the lonely intersections might hold two gas stations and a diner. The few frame-and-adobe houses seemed to have grown up from the ground.

One day, while driving in the New Mexico mountains, I pulled off the road in Hillsboro, a small, quiet town with a year-round population of about 150 people. Lydia Key, curator, welcomed me to the Black Range Museum. There I read that by 1880 Hillsboro had sprung to life as a gold-mining boomtown with four saloons, four grocery stores, four companies of soldiers, and a militia of 300 men to protect residents from outlaws and Apache raiders. I found a general store, bought a cold drink, and asked the woman behind the counter if any of the old claims were being worked. She nodded and casually told me that miners were finding gold in the nearby foothills of the Black Range. A hundred years ago, townspeople had probably thrilled to news of the latest strikes in Sierra County. Judging from the storekeeper's attitude, mining to her was little more than a curiosity.

To reach the goldfields, I turned onto a dirt road east of town and drove across parched scrubland. Suicidal jackrabbits darted in front of the van. In the distance, I saw fenced-off mine shafts and piles of tailings, those melancholy testaments to earlier attempts to mine the harsh, dry land.

In the course of the day, I met three miners. They were generally close-mouthed about their operations. One, as suspicious as a moonshiner, even asked that I not use his name or take his picture. He said darkly that he feared harassment from the federal government. The three mining operations, located in a dry arroyo known as Dutch Gulch, resembled highway construction sites because of the mounds of dirt and pieces of machinery scattered about. The men were engaged in placer mining, a technique that involves scraping the gold-bearing deposits—or placers—out of the streambed, and then extracting the gold by sending loose rock through a series of screens and washing it in a sluice box. Up until ten years ago, miners clawed at the ground with picks and shovels; today they rely on bulldozers that can tear up 500 cubic yards of dirt a day, in contrast to about four cubic yards using the hand method.

"This is like operating a gravel quarry," said Dave McCravey as he looked out the window of his mobile home at his bulldozed claim. "It's so different from what people think. It's deromanticized." Returning his eyes to his bookkeeping on the table before him, he added, "It's so hard to get the gold. It's very fine, and the good Lord scattered it over a large area. He didn't put it in puddles."

Of course, the thing that kept these men sweating in the sun was the extraordinary price of gold. During my visit it stood at $290 an ounce, a significant increase from the $35 of ten years before. (Several months later, the price catapulted briefly to $800 an ounce.) Despite these dizzying prices, gold fever was kept in check at Dutch Gulch. The operators usually maintained an impassive, businesslike air, with the fever showing only when someone heard the latest gold price on a radio.

Optimism necessarily runs in a deep vein with the miners. Jim McCants, a retired government worker, believed that mining gold would pay him more than his job ever did. "Whenever I've run a five-gallon bucket of dirt, I've found some gold," he said with pleased amazement. "I don't care where it was. It's all over." McCants, a lanky man who was working the same claim his uncle prospected in the thirties, was the most open of the miners. When I asked about his operation, which he had been running full time since 1974, he estimated that on a hard day he could "throw" forty cubic yards of dirt through the screens and sluice box, and come up with between one and one-and-a-half ounces of what he called "the yeller."

But the fabulous paydays have ended here. No longer will there be men like George Wells, a miner who, during the winter of 1877-78, carried some ninety thousand dollars in gold dust and nuggets into Hillsboro. That didn't stop Jim McCants from feeling excitement when he spotted color in his box. He smiled as if he had hit the jackpot on a slot machine.

The days have also passed when thumb-size nuggets would turn up in a sluice box. With prospectors scouring the area on and off for a hundred years, the easy pickings have vanished. In the last five years, McCravey had found just twenty nuggets, none larger than the head of a kitchen match. These modern miners sell minute particles about the size of fine grains of sand, stuff the early gold seekers had neither the technology nor the patience to bother with.

Inside a laboratory behind his house trailer, the man who preferred anonymity calmly spooned black sand from a sluice box onto a rotating water table—a kind of mechanical gold pan—and watched as yellow flecks separated from the concentrate. "There's your gold," he said with a chuckle. He hoped to make big money fast in Dutch Gulch.

McCravey, whose great-grandfather joined the California gold rush in the 1850s, entertained no such fantasies about making a quick fortune. "This is like farming," he said dryly of his one-man operation. "You build it gradually. Over a period of years you can make a good living at it. But if someone expects to get rich quick, he's crazy."

So people were toiling in the sun in the mountains of New Mexico, once again scratching for gold. McCants prospered after I saw him, adding his brother to the operation and buying more equipment. The man without a name, however, who was financed by a New York investor, folded his operation in the fall. Now the hot winds blow around his empty house trailer. Perhaps in a hundred years someone will spot the sagging, dust-coated structure and wonder if its owner ever struck it rich.

The next day I crossed the Continental Divide about fifty miles west of Hillsboro and soon imagined the highways running like rivers, carrying me inexorably westward toward the sea. The back roads thus became routes that led me out of the main flow and deposited me in unfamiliar country. So it was with a sense of exploration that I swung into the White Mountains of Arizona and crossed the Fort Apache Indian Reservation, bouncing over steep gravel roads traveled by loggers, ranchers, and, as I soon learned, by archaeologists.

West of the Apache village of Cibecue, while climbing through pine forests and across rangeland, I came upon a settlement of cabins and tents, home to twenty students, eight instructors, and eight staff members, all taking part in an eight-week archaeological field school sponsored by the University of Arizona. Their goal was to unearth and examine traces of the Mogollon, an Indian people who inhabited the area before Columbus discovered America.

On the afternoon I arrived at the camp, I tracked down a group of about 12 people hard at work excavating an oval pit house thought to have been used sometime around A.D. 900. A tarp slapped in the breeze above a series of rectangular holes where several young people were kneeling, meticulously scraping away dirt. The loose soil was being collected and run through a large sifter where the students checked for objects that might have been made or used by the Mogollon—a piece of charcoal, a fragment of pottery, a chunk of burned clay, a deer bone, a smoothed stone. The students were also trying to determine the outline of the structure. What looked simply like holes in the ground became

Fort Apache Indian Reservation   A sacred Sunrise Dance marks the passage
from childhood to womanhood for 13-year-old Janet DeClay, a White Mountain Apache in

Arizona. Accompanied by her best friend—her cousin Ronette DeClay—Janet holds a feathered cane, symbol of long life, and dances to chanted prayers, seeking strength and a healthy old age.

Arizona Highlands

In the rugged country of central Arizona, archaeologists uncover pre-Columbian pueblos and cliff dwellings of the Mogollon, Indians who roamed the Southwest for more than 1,500 years. At the Canyon Creek ruin, J. Jefferson Reid (right), director of the University of Arizona's archaeological field school, explores a 14th-century dwelling sheltered in the niche of a 200-foot bluff (left). Colleague H. David Tuggle (below) advises a team studying a twenty-room pueblo at Chodistaas as they seek clues to settlement patterns of the Mogollon.

Dirt-smudged and dig-weary, students Kristin Cheronis and Elizabeth Pate   *125*
conclude a day's excavations at a Mogollon site. "It's hard work," says Kristin,
holding a trowel, "but it's exciting when you have the end result in view."

potentially fascinating when Brian Byrd, supervisor of the pit-house excavation, explained how a large stone could indicate the level of the floor, or how a patch of orange-streaked clay might represent the location of the hearth, or how a curve in the hard earth might signify an outer mud wall.

As important as the discerning eye is to the archaeologist, it is a keen historical imagination that can justify the hours of tedious and painstaking rummaging in the dirt. Watching Kristin Cheronis working with a trowel as she traced a wall, I asked how she managed to retain her interest.

"A lot of people consider this hard work," she said, looking at me with a dirt-streaked face. "It's hard work, but it's exciting when you have the end result in view; when you can at last see larger patterns of organization." She kicked the dirt at her feet. "When we finally saw the outlines of this house, it didn't seem like so much work then."

While we were talking, a student at a nearby test hole held up a smooth rock the size of a fist and shouted, "Mano! Mano!" A mano was a tool used by the Mogollon for grinding meal. Members of the digging crew gathered to admire the find. Most of them offered a theory or two on what the location of the dusty stone signified, then returned to their trenches.

The pit house is a minor excavation compared with much of the work done at the field school since it opened in 1963. The main attraction has been the Grasshopper ruin, a 500-room pueblo in which possibly as many as a thousand people lived during the 14th century. It would have been among the largest dwelling places in the Southwest at the time.

Today the pueblo is a large, undramatic mound of earth strewn with rocks and overgrown with walnut and juniper trees. However, the straight lines of walls are still visible, the central plazas remain open, and a corridor exhibits expert sandstone masonry work. During 16 years of excavation, about a fifth of the rooms have been uncovered. Work has temporarily halted, according to field school director Dr. J. Jefferson Reid, to provide staff archaeologists an opportunity to analyze the material and write a report.

In the meantime, Dr. Reid has assigned students to find the earlier, more primitive pit houses in order to help determine the extent of Indian occupation in the area before the 14th century. "We're probably finished finding the impressive artifacts," he said. "We're now investigating the pattern of settlement and how people made a living in this rugged country hundreds of years ago."

A state grant supported the other major task of the summer: Students were surveying the general region around Grasshopper to identify the Mogollon and Apache sites and make recommendations on how to preserve them, especially against the persistent threat of pothunters.

One morning I joined Robbie Baer, Mary Dohnalek, Phil Jácome, and Michael Johnson in a search for a small pueblo known to exist in the area. Surveying, I found, is synonymous with hiking while keeping one's eyes trained on the ground. We were searching for what Mike called "Indian garbage": pottery fragments, or sherds, and pieces of worked stone known as lithics.

It is a camp joke for students, on spying a sherd or a lithic, to cry out, "I see wonderful things," a paraphrase of the words British archaeologist Howard Carter uttered in November 1922 when he looked into the splendid tomb of King Tutankhamun of Egypt. For three hours our survey team saw no wonderful things. On the ridges, we sighted only prickly pears, piñons, and dense clusters of the evergreen shrub manzanita, where rattlesnakes often hide. Despite the vigorous exercise and the marvelous pellucid air, we were a trifle dejected when we walked back toward the vehicle, at a loss as to how we had missed the site.

Then, fifty yards from the truck, near an Apache cornfield, I heard Mike cry, "Lithic!" And a second later, "Sherd!" We all stopped and began spotting a few bits of black-and-white pottery. We looked up from the ground, where our eyes had been glued, and saw a mound covered with brush and rubble. "Pueblo," we all shouted.

Mike and Phil sketched the chambers, recording their size and location. Apparently pothunters had beaten us to the spot, for the central area had been disturbed. Robbie and Mary, meanwhile, combed the site, counting about ten pieces of pottery in all. We returned to camp in high spirits, feeling our excursion had been a success.

I left the camp on a Sunday in mid-July, and for the next several days drifted through Arizona and into California, content simply to ride the roads on clear, hot summer days. On Friday, after driving through the furnace of Death Valley and crossing the Sierra Nevada through Walker Pass, I reached Mendota, population 4,145, a predominantly Mexican-American town in the San Joaquin Valley. Its population more than doubles in July, when transient field hands come to harvest the cantaloupe, tomato, lettuce, sugar beet, and cotton crops.

The afternoon I arrived, the town was nearly deserted, as most of the people were in the fields. By early evening, though, the streets began to fill. After all, it was a Friday night in summer, a time to loosen up and hang out. On Seventh Street, the town's main thoroughfare, people had collected on the sidewalks, standing outside the markets and bars, talking idly, relishing the advance of evening.

At seven o'clock the cars appeared. Heads turned to watch the row of highly waxed sedans, their frames lowered to within a few inches of the ground. They were moving slowly, very slowly, like floats in a parade. Only the parking lights were on, and disco music escaped from the windows. The drivers were sunk in their seats, their eyes barely clearing the steering wheels. Large brass plaques in the back windows read, "Masters of Illusions." Six cars in all glided down Seventh Street. They were cruising; the weekend had begun.

The cars and their drivers are known as "lowriders." Among young Mexican Americans in California, it has become popular to customize cars by lowering them as near to the ground as possible, lavishly decorating them inside and out, and driving them at 10 to 15 miles an hour in the classic weekend ritual of seeing and being seen.

For Ralph Aguero, 26, then the president of the Masters of Illusions, the basic reason is to exhibit one's "cool," or, in the slang of the

lowriders, to be "bad." "My aim is to have a bad car," Ralph told me on Friday night. "People, they see the car and they say, 'Check it out. That's a bad lowrider.' It makes me feel good. I like to show off. We don't want to speed. We like to take it low and slow."

After one pass through town, the Masters of Illusions gathered in the back room of a game arcade to hold a meeting. In the summer of 1979, the club included 25 members, all of them Mexican American except Buzz Rayfield, an Anglo. "I was into the hot rod trip, but it took too much gas," admitted Buzz, who works as a tomato inspector. "You get more people together with the lowriders. With hot rodders, it was everyone for himself."

Ralph, who is sensitive about the club's image in the community, emphasized that the Masters of Illusions enjoy an amiable relationship with the local police, to the extent that the police often escort the lowriders when they form a caravan to celebrate a wedding or some other social occasion. Alex Valdez, then the mayor of Mendota, is probably the club's staunchest supporter. Eager to encourage recreation among Mendota's young people, he helped acquire the back room of the arcade for the club.

Following the meeting, the Masters of Illusions returned to their cars. Naturally enough, the classiest vehicle belonged to Ralph. He owns what the others call a *firme ranfla*, a "real nice car." It is a sight. Ralph explained how he cut away coils on the springs of the 1974 Gran Torino to drop the body to the legal limit above the tire rims. He painted it a metallic candy-apple red—"It glitters in the sun," he says—and installed lights behind the grille and the chrome wheel rims. He added white shag carpet, a steering wheel made of chromed steel chain, a tape deck, and a television set. He has already spent $3,000 on

"Looking good!" Members of the Masters of Illusions lowrider club gather before

Mendota, California

Cruising "low and slow" provides both a pastime and a motto for Mexican-American "lowriders." With customized cars lowered to within inches of the ground, they drive the streets at a caravan's pace (left), protective of their cars (right)—but savoring the pleasures of seeing and being seen.

their cars; a trophy won in a parade crowns the club president's Gran Torino.

*H*igh class, lowrider-style: A show-car interior (left), complete with crushed-velvet trim, a television set, a tape deck, a welded-chain steering wheel, and leather-upholstered dash, doors, and seats, makes Ralph Aguero's lowrider "mean and clean." Club members at left, below, connect batteries that operate a hydraulic system—a hallmark of lowriders. With front and rear hydraulic lifts, a lowrider car can rear or buck like a horse, an attention-grabber that lures the amazed, the admiring, and sometimes the girls. Pausing on a Mendota street, Laura Garcia Castro and Paula Naranjo talk with lowrider James Beltrán (below). "If you take care of your car," says Ralph Aguero, former president of the club, "it will take care of you."

Flying low over fertile fields, a crop duster sprays farmland lush with summer- 133
greened sugar beets in the San Joaquin Valley, in California's agricultural
heartland. Massive water projects have transformed this once-dry region.

custom work and guesses he will need an additional $2,000 for the extra touches of putting a bar in the trunk, more crushed-velvet trimming inside, and a pair of heart-shaped seats in front.

Ralph invited me to ride with him as the Masters of Illusions once again eased down Seventh Street. When the caravan passed young women, the cars crawled even slower.

"Yes, a bad car will attract chicks," said Ralph, with the obligatory impassive face the club members assume. "I always say, if you take care of your car, it will take care of you."

At the end of the street, the cars, empty of females, pulled into the parking lot of a shopping center and arranged themselves in a row, the parking lights left on. Cases of beer were pulled from a few car trunks, and with the disco music throbbing, we toasted Friday night.

By now I had been traveling for six months and had covered 13,000 miles; to wake up in the morning, step into the van, and drive had become as natural a part of my day as winding my watch or brushing my teeth. My route now took me up the Sacramento Valley, where mile after mile of fruit orchards flashed by. Summer had deepened, and the afternoons took on a drowsy quality. I was now stopping for the night wherever the engine of the van overheated, as it invariably did on these hundred-degree days. Every morning, though, as if it were as eager as I to move on, the engine would roar to life, and I would resume my way.

This was the summer of dollar-a-gallon gas, and Skylab falling to earth, and a revolution in Nicaragua. But on the back roads, where the patterns of life can be so steady, the events of the world somehow became more remote with each passing day.

Headlines seemed especially irrelevant on the mountaintops in Klamath National Forest in northern California. Here dirt roads lead to the tops of 12 peaks where, for five months a year, lookouts live alone in towers, scanning the wilderness every waking hour, looking for the wisp of smoke that tells of fire. Up here, no news is good news.

Early one afternoon I visited Charles "Al" Frederickson at the lookout atop Lake Mountain, 6,903 feet high. For almost ten minutes after I arrived in his plainly furnished 14-by-14-foot room, Al didn't utter a word. He stood in the middle of his small quarters, staring through his green-tinted glasses like a sea captain at the helm of his ship. Finally, still absorbed in his job, the 67-year-old U.S. Forest Service employee spoke: "I keep my eyes moving, looking for smoke. If you're up here a long time, you get so used to the country that if something changes, you notice it."

What Al was vigilantly surveying was a spectacular panorama of forested mountains. Mount Shasta, at 14,162 feet, stands on the eastern horizon. This is breathtaking scenery that would inspire woolgathering or daydreaming in almost anyone, but the lookouts must remain alert. They stare at the vistas as if they were air-traffic controllers watching radar screens.

On the day I met Al, he was keeping an especially sharp eye on the

Klamath National Forest

"This country all around me is my big living room," says Nancy Culbertson, a fire lookout in northern California. From the door of her Eddy Gulch tower, she scans the horizon for fires (above). At left, a rainbow arcs above the forested slopes. Inside the tower, where she has worked as a lookout for 18 years, Nancy jots notes in a daily log (opposite). "Even though Eddy Gulch is isolated from city living, I meet people from all walks of life up here," she explains. "And I love to have visitors—the coffee pot is always on."

Pacific Northwest   *Huge logs of fir and hemlock loom behind mill worker Joe Cich as he sorts fresh-cut lumber at the Hanel Lumber Company, Inc., ten miles south of Hood River,*

Oregon. Forests blanket nearly half the state, which has led the nation in lumber production for forty years. The Hanel company produces some forty million board feet a year.

Clear skies draw stargazers to Goldendale Observatory in Washington.
Four amateur astronomers built the observatory's 24½-inch telescope.
Outside, staff members set up reflecting telescopes to view the heavens.

surroundings; a "condition red" had gone into effect, signifying a grave risk of fire. The area had had no appreciable rainfall for three months, and the forest was dry. An electrical storm the week before had touched off 22 small fires.

At Lake Mountain, Al, who has worked as a lookout for almost nine years, is responsible for about 117,500 "seeing acres," roughly a 15-mile radius from his tower. When he spots smoke, he goes to the center of the room to a firefinder, a circular map atop a metal column. Viewing the smoke through two small surveying sights, he takes an azimuth reading that tells him the location of the fire. He then promptly radios in his information. With readings from one or more other lookouts, the forest service personnel at the Yreka headquarters can pinpoint the fire.

Al prides himself on his vision. "He's picked up fires 15 miles away that were less than twenty feet across," said Al's boss, Ed Masonheimer, fire management officer of the Oak Knoll district where Lake Mountain is located. "Last year I spotted a fire 64 miles away," Al proudly recalled.

Surveillance has grown into an obsession with Al. "You're always looking. I don't care what time of day it is," he said. "You wake up at night, you twist and turn, you get up and look, and then go back to bed. This happens three or four times a night." Noticing some neatly stacked magazines on a desk, I asked if he squeezed in any reading. "I can read only a couple of paragraphs at a time," he answered. "You're always looking."

Generally, during the May 15 to October 15 lookout season, Al is allowed to go to his home in Yreka for two days out of a fortnight. When I saw him, however, he had not left the lookout for 19 days because of the fire hazard. He once remained for 54 days atop nearby China Peak. "It takes a special kind of person," observed Ed Masonheimer. "I'd wear a hole in the floor in thirty minutes."

Sometimes the isolation gets to a fire lookout. There is the story of a man in Sequoia National Forest in California who was nearly driven insane by a combination of isolation and an obsessive fear of ring-tailed cats scratching at the windows in the night.

"You have to be a person who likes to be by himself hour after hour," Al said, after hearing the story. "You don't want to put a person up here who needs to have people around him all the time." Despite this serene attitude, Al gratefully welcomes visitors. As I observed later, however, they sometimes interfere with his duties. Exactly 31 people had visited the tower so far during the season, Al told me. But the solitude doesn't bother Al; he's too busy looking.

Rapping his wooden desk, Al told me that he had reported no large fires thus far in the season. (Klamath National Forest escaped any major blazes in 1979.) I was able to witness Al in action, however. At about 3 p.m., Al agreed to pose for a picture on the tower deck. As Steve Hall, a friend of mine from San Francisco, was lining up a shot of Al staring to the south, Ed Masonheimer suddenly pointed to the east and yelled, "Al, there's a *hell* of a smoke over there."

Al hurried inside the tower, located the gray cloud on his fire-finder, and radioed in his report. The fire, which had already been reported by a closer station, was burning in a valley 34 miles away, near the Yreka airport. Calls had gone out for fire engines, a bulldozer, and two air tankers to drop fire-retardant chemicals. The blaze had been quickly contained by the fire engines, however, and the rest of the equipment was called off.

After the excitement, I apologized to Al for distracting him, and soon afterward left the mountain, feeling Al's eyes on me—"looking"—until I disappeared from sight.

Early in my travels, back in Maryland and North Carolina, whenever people asked me where I was headed, I often answered, "Alaska," just to see the surprise and wonder on their faces. Even in northern California, which is more in the neighborhood, my response still provoked a vivid reaction. For many people living in the lower forty-eight, Alaska carries the mystique of a place as distant and wild as a foreign country. If I had said I was destined for Panama or Peru, it would not have inspired the same animated response.

In late July, planning to ride a ship of the Alaska Marine Highway from Seattle to Alaska, I wound my way out of the mountains and entered foggy, chilly weather along the Oregon coast. After tarrying a few days in the vicinity of the Columbia River—visiting a lumber mill near Hood River, Oregon, stargazing at an observatory in Goldendale, Washington—I reached Seattle and boarded the M. V. *Matanuska*, bound for Alaska.

I stayed on board for almost three days, joining the 500 other passengers in a high-spirited vigil for bald eagles, bears, and whales, as the ferry crept up the inland straits. I disembarked at Sitka, the capital of Russian America in the first half of the 1800s, and, after witnessing a salmon run, flew on to Anchorage.

Once I arrived in Alaska, it did not take long to appreciate, in a most humble fashion, the immensity of the state. At dinner one night in Talkeetna, 113 miles north of Anchorage, photographer Ira Block and I were discussing our travel plans. We intended to run over to Eagle in the east, then dip southwestward to Homer on the Kenai Peninsula, and then scoot back to Anchorage.

The plan seemed manageable until Ira, noticing that the map scale indicated one inch for every hundred miles, instead of the ten or twenty miles we were accustomed to, quietly pointed out that Eagle was five inches away, and that for part of the way we would have to navigate

Scenes of rural beauty reward a back roads traveler: Rows of winter wheat pattern the land along a highway south of Goldendale, Washington.

a narrow, winding road over steep hills; we would be lucky to make our leisurely day-trip in two days. 141

Ira and I went on to discover—again meekly—that if we were to drive every mile of Alaska's roads, we would see only a minuscule part of the state. It would be like touring New York City and seeing only Central Park. (Alaska has about 9,700 miles of public roads; Massachusetts has more than 30,000, but Alaska is seventy times larger.) When we told Alaskans where we wanted to go, they automatically assumed we were flying.

The airplane far outranks the automobile as a practical means of transportation in Alaska. Many of the settlements in the state can be reached only by air or water. If Alaska has any back roads, they are the air lanes that bush planes fly to places like Bettles or Tanana. Even in Talkeetna, which is serviced by both a road and the Alaska Railroad, the airstrip is a busy place.

Ira and I drove to Talkeetna one day to talk with a bush pilot about flying the back roads. Talkeetna, we found, is a gathering place for climbers who have come to scale Mount McKinley and the numerous other mountains that dominate the sky northwest of town. On the day we arrived, 20,320-foot McKinley, the highest point in North America, was veiled in clouds, as it is more than half the time during the wet summer season. About 400 people live in and around Talkeetna, but the population had greatly swollen, as nearly a thousand people had flowed in to attend a weekend bluegrass festival at the baseball field next to the landing strip. Dancers were joyously stumbling through a Virginia reel when an orange-and-white Cessna 185 bounced down on the strip. Out stepped Cliff Hudson, a bespectacled man with dusty gray hair and a rugged, lined face. He was returning from his third unsuccessful attempt to drop food and fuel to four climbers who had been caught for five days in a snowstorm in dangerous avalanche country 16,000 feet up on the southeastern ridge of Mount Foraker, a slope near McKinley.

"Clouds too thick to see them," Cliff said, walking away from his plane. "I'll try one more time before the day ends."

Cliff Hudson is one of the finest pilots in Alaska. For almost thirty years he has been landing surveyors, trappers, hunters, and miners in the bush. His abiding interest, however, is in helping people on and off McKinley. Around town, Cliff enjoys an especially high reputation. In all his years of landing on the treacherous slopes of glaciers and flying in the thin air of high altitudes, where a plane needs a longer takeoff run, Cliff has not lost a passenger or a plane.

Pulling stories from Cliff was a major undertaking. He is a modest man who doesn't consider an action noteworthy if he performed it for a customer. He did talk a little, standing in front of the house where he lives with his wife and one of his four sons, Jay, also a pilot.

"I had to learn how to fly," he said, explaining how he came to buy his first plane in 1949. "It was the only feasible way to get around in Alaska at that time."

His brother then operated a flying service in Talkeetna. When the brother died in a plane crash in 1951, Cliff took over the business. "I hardly know from one day to the next what I'll be doing," says the man who carries a million-dollar insurance policy. "Some days I have to land on mountain trails, gravel bars, or (Continued on page 151)

Alaska   Dusk-gray clouds drape mountains along the shores of Turnagain Arm, a branch of Cook Inlet south of Anchorage. Tidal mud flats glisten between peaks of the Chugach and

Kenai mountains. Only 9,700 miles of public roads penetrate America's largest state, where flying often replaces driving, and airstrips service even the smallest wilderness communities.

Celebrating summer with a burst of song, dancers skip to a Virginia reel (opposite) at the annual bluegrass festival in Talkeetna, 113 miles north of Anchorage. News of the two-day gathering travels by word of mouth, attracting such bands as "Tanana Grass" (above) from Fairbanks. In 1979, a band composed of Swedish mountaineers who had attempted to climb Mount McKinley also performed. A combination of altitude sickness and bad weather had kept them from the summit. An easy pace marks life in Talkeetna, where businesses cater to climbers setting out to scale nearby Mount McKinley and, at right, hitchhikers off to explore the land.

Soaring on backcountry air lanes, Talkeetna bush pilot Cliff Hudson takes his Cessna 185 on a routine trip to pick up campers from a lake in the rugged Alaska Range (below). For thirty years, he has flown sportsmen, trappers, and surveyors in and out of Alaska's bush. In a Cessna equipped with ski wheels, he rescues climbers from the snow-packed slopes of Mount McKinley. Flying in thin air at 17,000 feet, he breathes oxygen (left) during a mission to drop supplies to climbers. Respected as a careful pilot, he has never lost a passenger or a plane.

"*Homesteaders have the best of two worlds,*" *says Yule Kilcher. "They take the minimum from civilization, and they don't add much to the problems." At his farm near Homer, a section of which he homesteaded in the 1940s, he clears trees (right), then pauses to play a hand-crafted flute; his dog Gypsy naps under the porch. Yule likens living without survival skills to going to sea without a lifeboat: "I've built a sort of raft here," he says. "Not Noah's Ark, just a raft."*

*W*histle-stop line for backwoods residents, the Alaska Railroad's AuRoRa train shuttles between Anchorage and Fairbanks, dropping mail and supplies to homesteaders along the way. During the busy summer season, passengers gather at the Talkeetna station, some returning to their wilderness settlements with fresh provisions. Piled by the tracks, a mound of gold-mining equipment represents someone's dream of finding more than solitude, beauty, or a new life in Alaska's frontier lands.

lakes." Cliff estimates that half his business comes from McKinley—flying sightseers around it, delivering mountaineers to the base camp at about 7,000 feet on the southeastern fork of the Kahiltna Glacier and picking them up again, and, on infrequent occasions, rescuing an injured climber.

Cliff's reputation is built not only on his safety record, but also on his consideration for his customers. He spent $4,000 staffing and equipping a base camp for his climbers, and usually flies over the trails to check a party's progress and condition.

It was during such a reconnaissance flight that Cliff was called upon to make one of his most dramatic rescues. "I happened to be in the plane when I heard on the radio that a climber was going into convulsions," he told me. "There had been 18 inches of new snow, so I radioed the boy's companions to trample down a runway for me with their snowshoes. My son brought my Piper Super Cub, which is equipped with ski wheels, to the base camp, and I took off and flew up to 14,500 feet. It was pretty rough. But as long as I know I can turn around, I'll go."

Flying over a dangerous precipice, Cliff landed on a slope where he had only 800 feet in which to stop. Picking up the climber, who was suffering from altitude sickness, Cliff then flew straight to Anchorage, delivering the passenger to an ambulance just as the boy was turning blue from lack of oxygen. "Afterward he wrote me a real nice letter," Cliff concluded. "He even sent me the fare."

The clouds had begun to lift as we talked, and soon Cliff excused himself for another attempt at making the airdrop to the climbers. Shortly afterward, Ira and I left Talkeetna. As we drove south out of town, the sun showered through the clouds, and in our rearview mirror, for the first time, we saw Mount McKinley filling the horizon. We hoped aloud that a small orange-and-white plane was hovering over one of the slopes near it. (We later learned that, despite the apparent clearing, clouds again foiled Cliff, but that the next day, on his fifth try, he accomplished his mission.)

Ira was driving, so I closed my eyes. The geography of the past two months had exhausted me. I had gone from the lowest point on the continent—Death Valley, 282 feet below sea level—to the highest, Mount McKinley. I had seen scorched scrubland and hardscrabble desert; cool, high forests and ocean-pounded coast. My route across the West, drawn on a map, resembled a string dropped on the floor, settling into random bends and curves. Yet the West, more than any other region of the country, it seemed to me, was too varied and too expansive for any traveler's string to tie up in a neat knot of explanation.

If there existed any common thread in my summer sweep, it was the people I met. They all seemed to be looking for something—for gold or oil, for smoke or mountain climbers, for remnants of the past. I was looking, too. As a traveler, I was searching for scenes that would stay in my mind—for people who, in the traveler's shorthand, would hint at an area's character. I was looking for excitement to kill the loneliness of the road. And finally, I was looking to the horizon, and ceaselessly moving toward it.

When I opened my eyes, I saw Anchorage at dusk, sprawled like a spilled deck of cards. Another day of travel was closing, another length of string had been dropped.

Autumn

SEPTEMBER CAME, and with a bug-spattered windshield I entered Montana. For two weeks I stayed close to the Rocky Mountains. To leave them and embark upon the Great Plains, which stretched before me like an open sea, would mean I was headed toward home, an eventuality for which I was not yet pre- pared. Despite occasional twinges of homesickness, the vision of a final destination unsettled me. I had grown attached to my nomadic existence, wandering the highways, free to go anywhere, passing in and out of people's lives with the impermanence of a weather front. Each day brought novelty—the narcotic of the traveler—and I was hopelessly addicted.

Unwilling as yet to answer the pull of homeward tides, I visited

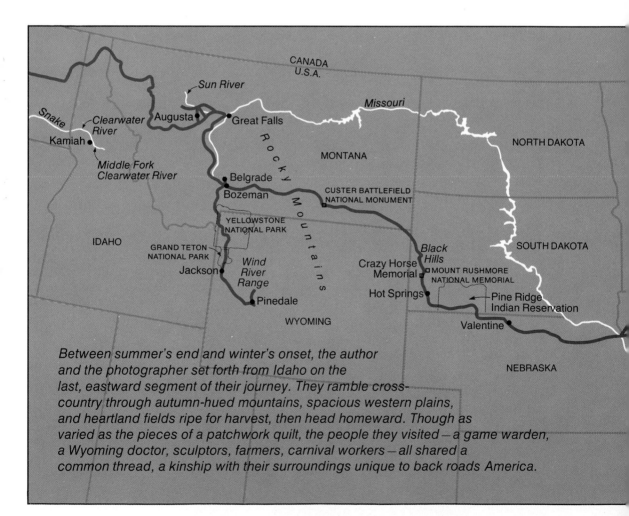

Between summer's end and winter's onset, the author and the photographer set forth from Idaho on the last, eastward segment of their journey. They ramble cross-country through autumn-hued mountains, spacious western plains, and heartland fields ripe for harvest, then head homeward. Though as varied as the pieces of a patchwork quilt, the people they visited—a game warden, a Wyoming doctor, sculptors, farmers, carnival workers—all shared a common thread, a kinship with their surroundings unique to back roads America.

such people as Paul Mihalovich, a Montana game warden for a 4,500-square-mile district that extends from the wheat fields and cattle estates west of Great Falls to the mountains along the Continental Divide—an area almost as large as Connecticut. These mountains are home to grizzly bear, elk, and bighorn sheep, and I hoped to catch a glimpse of the wildlife while the warden reconnoitered his province. During our two days together, I listened to stories of fields thick with bighorns, of the autumn migration of thousands of elk from the snowy highlands, of grizzlies raiding local farms for livestock, and even of an alleged ape-like creature named Bigfoot.

The only creature I saw, though, was a pronghorn buck standing in the middle of the road. Hearing our truck approach, he waved his white, cottony behind and sprinted across the grassland. I also saw a busload of young geophysicists and geologists from Denver. Hammers in hand, they were looking for evidence of mineral deposits. They conjured up images of oil and gas companies drilling in the mountains. Warden Mihalovich fears for this wilderness. "Can't we realize that this land is infinite, while we're here for only a second?" he muttered.

I joined autumn crowds touring Yellowstone and Grand Teton National Parks. One day late in the afternoon I saw by the side of the road a large elk, its rack as sizable as a tree bough, gingerly crossing a creek. Spotting wildlife near the road in these parks is not terribly

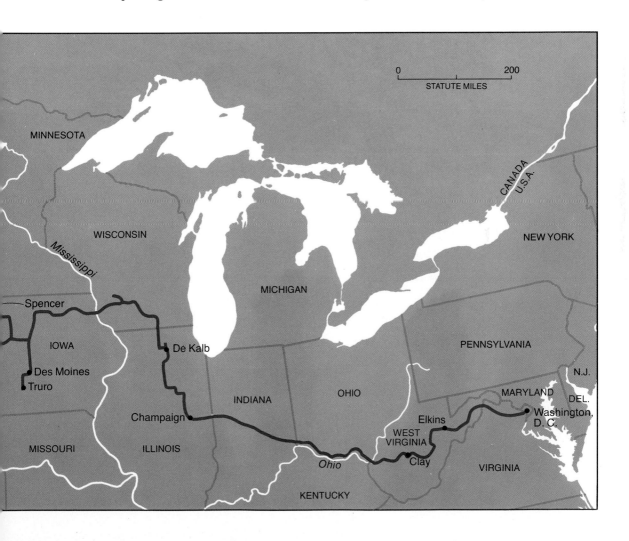

difficult. A line of cars, brake lights flashing and camera lenses poking out of windows, lets an approaching driver know there's something to be seen. I am an unabashed gawker in these situations. My heart jumped when I saw the elk, a harmonious sight in its forest setting. If there was anything unnatural or obtrusive about the scene, it was us—the occupants of noisy, idling cars.

While still near the mountains I met Judie Tallichet, a young sculptor who lives in a small gray farmhouse outside Bozeman. Schooled as a sculptor in her home state of Kentucky, Judie migrated to Montana, where she is finding her "artistic purity." Using shapes and materials natural to the Montana countryside, she has turned the whole outdoors into her gallery, constructing giant willow hoops and timothy-grass arches in nearby fields. She explains that she is exploring ways that art can fit naturally into the landscape, and at the same time heightening her perception of her surroundings.

Besides pursuing her own projects, Judie spends ten months each year working for Artists in Schools. This program, funded jointly by Montana and by the National Endowment for the Arts, hires writers, painters, sculptors, and filmmakers to visit the state's many rural schools and introduce the children to art. One day I accompanied Judie to a white frame one-room schoolhouse near Belgrade. For her workshop, she would ask the students to create sculptures out of sticks and twine and to position the finished work outdoors. The lesson was meant to stretch the children's concept of art. "Too often children consider art to be what their parents hang above the sofa," she said as we rumbled along in her vintage 1952 GMC pickup.

In most cases, the rural children are receptive to her ideas about environmental art, Judie said. "I'm delighted by the honesty and unpretentiousness of the farm kids," she told me. "Naturally they don't understand my sculptures right away, but if I introduce them to tools that are familiar and lay a groundwork so they can see things differently, maybe later they will understand why I do what I do."

When we drove up to the gate of the schoolhouse, the student body of 11 was waiting on the front stoop. The school is set in a valley in the Rockies, amid fields of wheat and alfalfa. Thin, dark-haired Judy Salisbury led us inside to the room where she teaches eight grades. To stimulate ideas, the guest artist spent several minutes showing slides of what other students had created for their projects—gigantic hay bales, an automobile manufactured from willow branches, a buffalo drawn with stones carefully placed on the slope of a hill. Judie then produced a roll of twine and a few cans of paint and, pointing outside, said, "Build me a sculpture."

For two hours the students scattered around the schoolyard, cheerfully climbing trees, pawing through piles of fallen limbs, sawing, clipping, and snapping until they had collected their sticks. They then retreated to separate patches of shade where they assembled their objects, while Judie walked among them lending encouragement and advice. Next they gathered at the steps and liberally applied paint, not

Bathed in light, a small grove hugs a bend of U.S. 12, just west of Kamiah, Idaho. Here, steep evergreen-forested slopes enclose the narrow road; farther south it follows curves of the Middle Fork of the Clearwater River.

Belgrade, Montana

Afternoon lesson in environmental art brings students of Springhill School out to forage for willow and cottonwood limbs. Guided by visiting artist Judie Tallichet (above, at left), children at the one-room school create fanciful figures from the simple materials they gather from neighboring meadows and woods. They then arrange the stick figures in groups and place them around the schoolyard. A sculpture can express "a thought of life," as one child explained, or represent a purely imaginary being.

To 12-year-old Charity Berendes, a bumpy branch (left) suggested a dragon, needing only a cap made of newspaper, a necktie of string, and spots of tempera "just to add color and contrast." Affixing a last bit of tape, first graders Jessica Mangas and Jenny Wagner (above, right) complete the "Dancing Lady." Jessica feels a special affection for "Sally" (right), long-haired friend of Jenny's dancer.

Augusta, Montana

On duty at sunrise, game warden Paul Mihalovich discusses the year's slow hunting season with game checkers Bud Bisnett and Odin Neckstad. Mihalovich patrols a 4,500-square-mile game district in the western part of the state, enforcing hunting regulations and providing information to sportsmen. At left, Thomas Brewster, wearing the mandatory hunter-orange, trades information on game sightings with Mihalovich after presenting his license for inspection. Impounded evidence to be sold at public auction, a whitetail buck (right), shot on a preserve, cost a hunter a $100 fine.

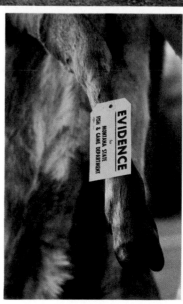

only to the pieces, but also to the grass and to their clothes. Finally the sculptures were placed on the grounds, and one by one the shy but excited children explained their creations.

There was a man with a pinecone head climbing a fir tree, a raft and a canoe bobbing in the creek behind the school, a large stick man seated at a rusting hay rake in an alfalfa field. Also in the fragrant field was a wooden horse with a painted slab of bark for a face. It looked like a prehistoric talisman found in a canyon cave.

Judie was pleased with the results. The children had associated art with pleasure and imagination and had used materials they had found right at their feet.

Before leaving the mountains, I drove to the small Wyoming town of Pinedale. It would be a pleasure to live here if only because one can walk to its southern edge, look to the east, and there see the Wind River Range, perhaps the most glorious collection of mountain peaks in the United States. One of the best vantages is the hill where the new medical clinic sits. There I met Dr. J. T. Johnston, the town physician. In fact, he is the only full-time man of medicine within a 35-mile radius of Pinedale. Doctor Tom, as he is known, is a balding, middle-aged man with a frank, uncompromising nature. The mountains he sees from his window remind him of a story.

Twenty-three years ago, as an Easterner who had come from Pennsylvania with his wife and a medical degree, Tom had been Pinedale's doctor for only a few weeks when two cowboys came to his house and asked him to come help an injured woman. The young doctor quickly packed his medical bag and accompanied the cowboys to an outlying ranch. When they arrived, he could barely conceal his surprise when he was invited to sit down to a large supper. During the meal, all Doctor Tom could think of was a woman lying injured somewhere. When he finished eating, Tom was even more surprised to be called outside and told to mount a horse that had been saddled for him. The two cowboys, with the doctor between them, rode off into the mountains in the darkness. Tom, who had not been on a horse in many years, clutched the reins tightly and passed up the whiskey that was being handed back and forth.

Early in the morning, the threesome reached the injured person—a woman from Nebraska who had shattered her hip in a fall. The doctor prepared a splint, rigged the patient to a stretcher, and had her carried out of the mountains. He flew to a Denver hospital with the woman, and by the end of the week the name of this freshly transplanted doctor from the East had made the local papers.

Now little surprises Doctor Tom. With no hospital to back him up—the nearest ones are in Jackson, 75 miles to the northwest, and Rock Springs, a hundred miles south—he must treat all manner of cases, from heart attacks and broken arms to bloody noses and dog bites. He still makes house calls to ranches as much as forty miles away. His rescue work in the mountains has slackened, though; helicopters have replaced him there.

On the day I observed him at work in the year-old clinic (he had previously operated out of a log house that at one time had been a dance hall), Tom treated a wide variety of cases, as is customary. He looked at an injured jaw, a sprained knee, a leg ulcer, and a lacerated lip. He set a fractured leg, diagnosed appendicitis, checked a woman who had had a miscarriage the previous week, and prescribed medicine for a sore throat.

During the examinations, Doctor Tom didn't wear the standard white coat and stethoscope because he doesn't like to intimidate his patients. He prefers to relax them with a mixture of teasing and comforting. "I like relations with my patients to be informal," he explains. "I don't want children to cry when they see me on the street."

His manner is distinctly unsugared, though. A distraught rancher's wife, expecting a child at the Rock Springs hospital, telephoned to say that another doctor had warned her of the possibility of a premature birth and recommended she transfer to Salt Lake City for more specialized care. She told Doctor Tom that she couldn't afford to go to this other hospital, and besides, she hadn't experienced any trouble with her other births. "Trust the doctor and spend the extra money," Doctor Tom told her firmly. "Just tell your husband to sell a few more cows. You can always raise new cows, but you can't always help a baby that's been damaged."

Being the one doctor in a small, semi-isolated town provides Tom with a certain privileged, almost priestly, status. Not only does he fill the conventional role of healer, but he also serves as confidant, adviser, and sometimes conscience to members of the community. Few secrets are kept from the town doctor.

Tom makes three or four house calls a week. The number was larger before a volunteer county paramedic squad and a county health nurse began answering emergency calls. "More doctors would make house calls if people didn't overdo it," he said. "When people in this county say they want to see you, they mean it. In my 23 years, it's never been abused." The two major drawbacks to a rural doctor's job, Tom said, are the lack of professional peers and the taxing work load. "While it may look like I'm relaxed here at home talking with you, actually I'm waiting for the phone to ring," he told me. Sure enough, minutes later the phone rang, and he was called upon to reopen the clinic for a woman who had been accidentally struck on the head.

By the time he finally sat down to dinner, Dr. Johnston was weary. He admitted that the constant responsibility of his work exhausted him and that occasionally he yearned for an eight-to-five job. He can no longer find time to ride the horse he keeps in his yard or to work on the ranch he recently bought outside town. Yet, after voicing this lament, Tom confessed that he never takes long vacations because he doesn't like to feel dispensable.

After dinner, the normally dispassionate doctor became sentimental. He remembered times when, as a young doctor, he would be driving back to Pinedale after delivering a baby at the Rock Springs hospital. "When I'd see the sun coming up over the Wind River Range, I'd say to myself, 'God meant for me to take care of the people in this valley.'" He laughed, embarrassed by his emotion.

The leaves of the hardwoods were yellowing when I finally left the mountains and pointed the van east. The radio was on: "Guess the time and date of the first freeze in Great Falls and win cash," a disc jockey was saying. In the Great Plains, roads cut across the landscape like strokes in an abstract painting. I drove through rolling grasslands and passed the Custer Battlefield National Monument, where in June 1876 Sioux warriors wiped out Lt. Col. George Armstrong Custer and units of the Seventh Cavalry.

Western Montana   *Early morning sun warms a late November landscape in the valley of a branch of the Sun River two miles east of Augusta. Brushed with new snow, the*

Rocky Mountains loom in the distance. The house, built in 1885 by a settler from New Hampshire, lies within a game preserve. The same family of ranchers has occupied it since 1898.

The next day I reached the Black Hills of South Dakota and found, 17 miles from the famed Mount Rushmore National Memorial, a mountain called Thunderhead. It appeared strangely ravaged. The southern side had a blasted look, and its contour was radically uneven. For two days I stared at the mountain. Gradually I began to see the rough outline of an arm pointing east across the plains, a stallion's head thrown wildly to one side, and the noble profile of a man looking into the distance. What the beat-up mountain turned out to be, almost unbelievably, was a sculpture-in-progress. Its subject is Crazy Horse, the legendary Sioux chief who helped destroy Custer's command at the Little Bighorn. When the massive project is completed—and no one knows when or if that will be—it will be the world's largest sculpture.

When I arrived, a small crowd had collected on a viewing porch about a mile from Thunderhead to witness a dynamite blast. Right on schedule, what looked like a wisp of dust bloomed near the flattened crown of the mountain, followed by a tremendous booming that rolled down the slope and bounced amid the surrounding hills. When the smoke cleared, the mountain seemed unchanged.

Grandiose dreams necessarily contain elements of fervor and obsession, and the man responsible for changing a mountain, 71-year-old Polish-American sculptor Korczak Ziolkowski, is not one to minimize the drama of his undertaking. "Out of four and a half billion people on earth, I'm the only man alive who's trying to carve a mountain," he said. "Since man's been on the planet, no pharaoh, no king, no government, no combination of people has attempted to make a sculpture of this proportion." For the past 31 summers, Korczak has been using unorthodox carving tools—dynamite, air hammers, and bulldozers—to create a sculpture 563 feet high and 641 feet long.

I met Korczak when he came off the mountain in the afternoon. He is a tall, brawny man. With his leathery face and a long, flowing gray beard that shakes when he talks, he resembles the Moses that his idol, Michelangelo, carved. Korczak was obviously tired when his wife, Ruth, who acts as his liaison with the public, helped him pull off his dusty, sweat-soaked denim shirt. But a couple of Manhattans and the prospect of telling his story yet again gradually revived him. He needs publicity. The money to create the Crazy Horse monument comes largely from the four dollars each carload of tourists pays to view the working area and to visit Korczak's gallery and museum of Indian artifacts. In 1979, some 650,000 people came to see the mountain. Twice, in 1951 and 1963, he turned down financial help from the federal government; he doesn't want anyone altering his vision.

In a voice edged with the accent of his native Boston, Korczak speaks with an oratorical flourish, running through a scale of attitudes. At one moment, he may appear sentimental and meditative; at another, arrogant and combative. Yet whatever twists the conversation may take, it always returns to what he calls, "my mountain."

A self-taught artist who learned to carve while working in the Boston shipyards, Korczak had become a successful sculptor by 1939, when he won a prize at the New York World's Fair. That same year he was hired to assist sculptor Gutzon Borglum in the carving of Mount Rushmore. While working there, Korczak received a letter from Henry Standing Bear, a Sioux chief at the nearby Pine Ridge Indian Reservation and a relative of Crazy Horse. Having watched the faces of Presidents Washington, Jefferson, Lincoln, and Theodore Roosevelt take

Pinedale, Wyoming   As the only physician for a remote ranching
community, Dr. Tom Johnston still makes house calls on patients unable to reach his clinic.
He greets "short and feisty" Raymonde Sell at her front door with good-natured banter.

At the approach of winter, Doctor Johnston makes his annual visit to a Northwest Pipeline compressor station to conduct a flu-shot clinic. As company doctor, he feels "a responsibility to keep the workers healthy during the months most critical for heat and gas production." Driving 55 miles through desolate sagebrush country in his pickup (below), he arrives in time for the 7 a.m. shift change. Amid lighthearted heckling, he vaccinates district superintendent "Skeet" Biggs as colleague Dale Swan checks him off the list (right). A stop for coffee and doughnuts at the Sage Cafe on the way back to Pinedale (left) affords Doctor Johnston yet another visit with old friends.

"*To provide 24-hour coverage, the only time you are 'off call' is when you're out of town,"* says Doctor Johnston, describing a life constantly monitored and interrupted by radio communications with his office. At the county-owned clinic he operates in Pinedale, Johnston treats many trauma cases, not unusual for an area with high-risk jobs in oil and gas production, ranching, and heavy construction. Much of his practice involves children, with whom he feels a special rapport.*

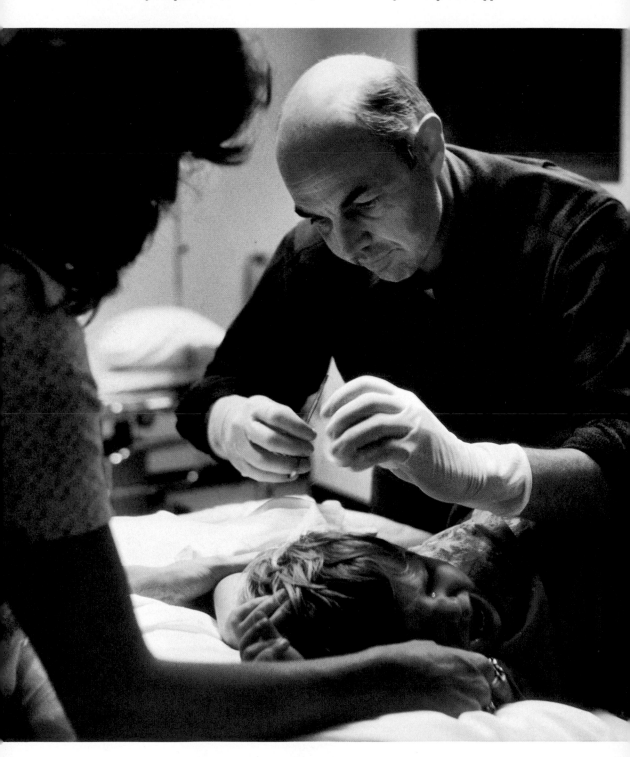

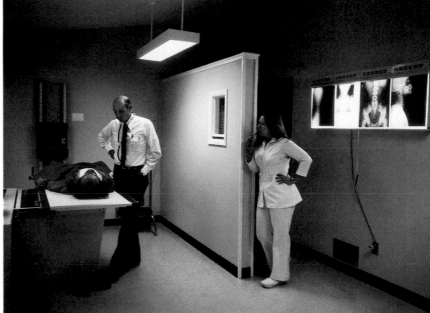

*Late evening emergency: Three-year-old George Licking, Jr., has
fallen and cut his head. While reassuring the mother, Doctor
Johnston readies sutures for his patient. Above, Johnston helps
ambulance attendants wheel another accident victim—Hal
Glanville, who fell from the roof of his house—into the clinic for
examination and X rays. Together with his nurse, Peggy Weber, the
doctor explains to Glanville that he may have fractured his neck.*

shape, Henry Standing Bear had conceived the idea of honoring the American Indian. In the letter, the aging chief proposed a mountain memorial to Crazy Horse. He wrote: "My fellow chiefs and I would like the white man to know that the red man had great heroes too."

"I didn't answer the letter," Korczak recalls. "I was quite surprised. I hadn't met any Indians in South Dakota. I hadn't even heard of Crazy Horse." When a second letter came, Korczak found himself becoming interested in the project. "This Indian barely had enough to eat, yet he wanted me to carve a mountain to a great chief. I was intrigued. I bought his dream."

K orczak, who describes himself as a "crusader for lost causes," began delving into American history. "The treatment of the Indians is the blackest mark on the escutcheon of America," he now concludes. "As I once told a federal official, I'd like to be the kind of white man who does what the Indians want."

In 1946, Korczak and Henry Standing Bear scouted the Black Hills until they found a mountain suitable for carving. On June 3, 1948, Korczak sealed his commitment. With members of the Sioux nation standing by—including five Indians who had fought in the Battle of the Little Bighorn—the first blast of dynamite sounded on the mountain. Since then, Korczak has almost single-handedly blasted six and a half million tons of granite from the mountain—about 15 times the amount removed from Mount Rushmore.

One morning I joined Korczak as he worked. The view from Thunderhead takes in a breadth of hills, valleys, and plains—the sacred ground of the Sioux. In addition to South Dakota, parts of Wyoming and Nebraska can be glimpsed from this vantage. As we drove up the road that Korczak has hacked out, he dramatized the dimensions of his work: 4,000 people could stand on Crazy Horse's arm when it is completed; all of the sixty-foot-high heads on Mount Rushmore could fit inside the Indian's head; a five-room house could be squeezed into one of the horse's nostrils.

At the top of the mountain, three of Korczak's sons—Adam, Joel, and Casimir—were drilling holes for the next dynamite charge. (Korczak, father of ten, also has five daughters helping manage the tourist operation at the base of the mountain.) While his sons drilled, the imposing old man stepped aboard a fifty-ton D9 Caterpillar tractor and proceeded to clear the slopes of boulders loosened by an earlier blast. Up close, it was impossible to see any of the sculpture's inchoate features. But as Korczak jounced over boulders and ran his machine to the very edge of cliffs, he shouted that he was clearing away the space around the horse's head. "I've been waiting to do this for years," he yelled.

Always he is asked when he will finish. "I usually tell people that if I can have six or seven more years, you'll be able to drive up the highway and see an Indian on a horse." He freely admits that he will not live long enough to finish the project, but he hopes to leave at least a more discernible outline. He has placed in a vault his calculations and measurements for the completion of the mountain, and he and his wife have been looking for someone to pick up the work when Korczak dies.

These days, Korczak feels very mortal. His body aches. Over the years, while working on the mountain, he has suffered two heart attacks; had five disks removed from his back; broken a wrist, ribs, and a thumb; and damaged his hearing and his eyesight. His arthritis is so bad he grimaces when he works the levers of his bulldozer. In 1979, he finished building himself a tomb at the base of the mountain.

Korczak is, by turns, a sensitive dreamer, a leather-skinned pioneer, a forceful crusader, an embattled artist. But always it is the artist he falls back on. "I'm a storyteller in stone," he says.

Back on the road, I drove southeastward into Nebraska. There is a hypnotic quality in the long, even stretches of the Midwest, and for almost three days I found myself driving practically nonstop. A procession of utility poles marched along the road, mile-long trains glided in the distance, and whirling windmills stood alone in spacious fields. Having grown up in the Midwest, I feel a certain loyalty toward not only its people, but also its topography. Many times I have insisted to friends from other regions of the country that endless miles of cornfields can be beautiful, that flatness has an appeal of its own. Occasionally, though, as on a warm September afternoon of driving for three or four solid hours across Nebraska or Iowa, I will concede that a straight-edged landscape can be monotonous. The car radio was invented for just such times.

"KIMM—Rapid City. Bringing you the best of the West." There was no end to the country-and-western songs on the radio. Station after station played twangy tunes about heartbreaks and split-ups and bittersweet memories. "Next is Jimmy Dean singing 'Sweet Misery.'" I couldn't listen to much, having broken up a few weeks earlier with a longtime girlfriend. Each song seemed to be dedicated to me.

I punched a button. "The Peabody Hale Show from KOBH, Hot Springs." A song: *Let's all go down to the river; there's a man walking on the water.* Plenty of religious shows preached at me. A host on a Christian call-in show was taking comments on the quality of television programming. "I think 'Charlie's Angels' is the work of Satan," one caller declared, fury in her voice.

Voices, voices—urging me to buy a combine or a snowmobile, reporting loins and hams steady on the Chicago market, forecasting a warm, sunny day. Punch the buttons. The Mets are beating the Cubs two to nothing in the third inning. Punch. "Valentine firemen this afternoon put out a basement fire caused by a faulty clothes dryer. Two escapees from a correction home are apprehended by . . ." Punch. "You have been listening to the Beethoven Piano Sonata No. 31 in A Flat." Punch. "Gold hit a record $349 on the London market . . . the Midwest grain handlers' strike has been settled . . . Edward Kennedy today lashed out at President Carter. . . ." Punch.

I always ended up listening to the Top 40. Half a dozen noisy tunes might go by, but suddenly there would come a favorite, one I knew the words to. The utility poles kept time. I sang loudly, and there was no need to stop; movement was rhythm, free and easy. I loved those moments of riding an airwave. But finally quiet was needed, and the radio would go dark. It was a decent companion. I sang to it, scoffed at it, laughed, applauded, and snorted. I could always change the subject or tell it to hush. And the miles kept passing by.

I halted in Iowa to visit a back roads celebrity by the name of Joe Hays. A few months earlier, while watching the evening news on television, this 39-year-old farmer heard that Pope John Paul II was coming to the United States for a week in the fall.

A few days later, Joe impulsively wrote to the Pope and invited him

Black Hills

With six and a half million tons of granite blasted away, the rough shape of the Crazy Horse Memorial begins to emerge from Thunderhead Mountain in South Dakota. If completed, the monument to the American Indian (seen in a scale model at left) will stretch 641 feet and rise 563. Its creator, Korczak Ziolkowski, gave up a career as a sculptor in Boston in 1946 to pursue a dream impossible to realize in his lifetime. On the door of the tomb he built for himself, he asks to be remembered simply as a "Storyteller in Stone."

Raising clouds of dust, two of Korczak's sons drill holes for dynamite charges near the horse's left eye. They must blast another million tons of granite from the mountain before the shape of the horse's head will be complete, Korczak says.

to stop in Iowa to see America's heartland. To the amazement of everyone who knew about the letter, the Pope accepted. So Joe Hays made the news—over and over again. He estimated that he had given almost 300 interviews. The fact that a midwestern farmer could influence the world head of the Roman Catholic Church aroused the melodramatic instincts of editors and producers across the country. This was a made-to-order human interest story. See, there *is* good news out there, the media could proclaim.

Curious to see how a back roads phenomenon would be treated by the media, I timed my visit for the day a crew from ABC's "Good Morning America," a morning news-and-information show, was to film the Joe Hays story. When I arrived at the ninety-acre farm near Truro, Joe was driving a tractor. Straddling the engine in front was a man pointing a TV camera at him. Take one: the farmer at work.

When this scene-setting shot was finished, Joe and his wife, Ann, joined me in the front yard and offered me a glass of iced tea. Joe was dressed in faded blue jeans and a short-sleeved work shirt. A farmer's cap covered his close-cropped dark hair. During the week, he works as a mechanic on experimental farm implements at a John Deere plant. He had taken a day's leave for the network filming.

"I knew I had a nice story to tell," Joe told me, in his sincere, enthusiastic manner. "My barometer was the people at work. By their interest I knew that my letter and the Pope coming to Iowa was a pretty big thing." Joe, a devout Catholic who, as a high school sophomore, attended Mass 363 days in one year, was obviously pleased by all the attention. "My hardest work was for *People* magazine," he recalled. "The photographer had me harvesting cucumbers and cabbage in the garden. I was working harder than I usually do."

A gray sedan soon pulled into the yard, and out breezed Sandy Hill, one of the hosts for "Good Morning America." She cut a figure in the Iowa farmland. Dressed in designer jeans, expensive cowboy boots, a billowy orange chiffon blouse, and a suede vest, she swept through our small crowd like a summer storm, shaking hands, kissing cheeks, squeezing shoulders. Just in from New York City, she was irrepressibly friendly and energetic. Only Joe Hays had a broader smile.

In the house, the crew set up the camera and lights. While Hays children peered from the kitchen doorway, Joe sat at the head of the table under a large crucifix on the wall. Sandy Hill was leaning forward on her elbows, looking intently at him. The camera rolled and Sandy asked how he felt, *really* felt, about this and that. Unabashed and relaxed, Joe told how his pride in the Iowa farm country and his concern about the global food situation had prompted him to invite the Pope. He said that everything in his life was now directed toward meeting the Pope when he arrived by helicopter in a few weeks to conduct Mass in a field outside Des Moines. Asked how his sudden fame had affected his life, Joe answered simply that his days were busier, he was receiving more mail, and there were new faces in church.

During a break, I asked the producer, Phyllis McGrady, why the media had become so intrigued by small-town stories. "I'm finding really interesting stories out in places like this," she told me. "Before, the networks all covered the same things in the same places. Statistics show that viewers like the 'real people' story—features about people they can identify with; not people at, say, Studio 54 in New York. The viewers can feel that they are a part of the story—part of Joe Hays."

"It's a slice of Americana, a piece of humanity," Sandy Hill said, warming to the subject. "The viewer can see something different, can see people living in the country. I see these stories as opportunities to touch people. What I like to do is show the positive aspects of life, the celebration of life."

I began to understand that small-town life has taken on a symbolic importance to city dwellers. As seen from the metropolis, life in the country probably seems simpler, more virtuous, more attuned to rhythms that city people think they are out of step with. Feature stories from these out-of-the-way places are like postcards sent to the big city, or samplers hung on 19-inch screens. The rural subjects scratch their heads and wonder what all the fuss is about. Yet apparently these light, deliberately wholesome pieces have a positive effect on urban audiences. They can believe that things aren't so bad after all. How much is truth and how much is delusion in this notion is impossible to tell. Cut. Commercial.

A few weeks later, in an Iowa field, Joe Hays met Pope John Paul II and shook the Pontiff's hand. They talked about farming and the Hays family for several minutes. Later, at the outdoor Mass celebrated by the Pope, the Iowa farmer participated in Holy Communion. For Joe Hays, this was prime time.

As I traveled roads through the rich farm country of northwestern Iowa, a sequence of sights kept repeating itself: a town sign, grain elevators, a water tower, a grocery store, a row of frame houses, fields of soybeans and corn, a cluster of farmhouse, barn, and silo, a town sign, and so on. Outside Spencer, the seat of Clay County, there predictably came into sight the grain elevators and the water tower, but there was something different here, something moving, revolving, outlined in lights. It was a Ferris wheel. I had arrived during a county fair.

For three days I submerged myself in it. After weeks of visiting small towns, I found something almost cosmopolitan about the fair, with its lights and noise and entertainment. An official, Myles Johnson, provided some facts. Every year, the Clay County Fair attracts an average of more than 250,000 people during its eight-day run. It is the largest district fair in the state, and it contains one of the largest displays of farm machinery in the country.

Yet, a fair is a fair. There are the barns, and there is the midway. The fair is a festival for people from towns, farms, and one-street villages of the county. They come together to enjoy themselves and to hurrah their way of life.

Daylight hours at the fair were spent in the barns. Here, on the west side of the fairgrounds, youngsters from 4-H clubs and the Future Farmers of America had brought the cattle, pigs, and sheep that they had raised. They now hoped to win some ribbons. On the day of the judging, a brisk, businesslike air ruled the 4-H cattle barn. The children and their parents were grooming the cud-chewing entries—scrubbing, brushing, combing, trimming, and drying. I doubt that the cattle ever looked better than when they were led into the show-ring by their serious-faced guardians.

After the judging, the mood relaxed in the cool shadows of the barn. While the animals lay down, the youngsters lounged on equipment boxes and hay bales or stood around in the aisles. There was horseplay in front of one stall; boys and girls were flirting in a corner. 177 Some children were eating sandwiches with their families. Others were jawing with friends. Fresh hay tanged the air; ribbons were thumb-tacked to the stalls. This was the heart of the fair.

Another congregating spot was the machinery display lot. Spread across 18 acres were rows of new, brightly painted farm implements—tractors, combines, plows, cultivators. The machines were so large and numerous that it was easy to imagine the earth being subdued. Pennants of the different manufacturers flapped overhead. In the John Deere area was a combine, a leviathan going for $115,000. Farmers were climbing around on it as if it were a jungle gym.

"There's a lot of wishing going on," one farmer said as he observed the action. Another remarked, as he investigated a tractor: "I just came to see how ridiculous the prices are."

"Five percent of the farmers are dead serious, ready to buy. Another 40 percent might get the fever," a salesman calculated. The young farmers appeared to be expending more serious, hand-in-chin looks than the old-timers. But almost everyone was trying out a seat on a tractor or combine. Dreaming is debt-free.

After eavesdropping in the machinery lot, I walked through the commercial-exhibit buildings. The effect was like watching a continuous television commercial. Booth after booth heralded some indispensable product, from fertilizer and gravestones to food blenders and the Democratic Party. Upstairs in one building I found the 4-H vegetable display. Tomatoes and squash and peppers appeared as bright and plump as those in a European street market. Rye and millet grasses were tied in handsome sheaves. All about was a cornucopia.

Some of the most dramatic moments of the daytime fair occurred at the beef auction. Boys and girls who had raised their animals like pets now saw them turned into products. "A dollar thirty-five," cried a buyer in the bleachers as he made the winning price-per-pound bid on a 1,165-pound steer in the show-ring. A fair official shouted, "This one goes to Spencer Foods," a slaughterhouse that would process it. Finally, a truck pulled up and took the animals away. Some of the younger children cried. Money had not yet cut through their sentimentality. Near the end of the auction, I saw one teenage girl looking over the rails of a pen as her newly sold steer butted heads with another. When her animal wandered alone into a corner and began to bellow mournfully, the girl quickly turned away and disappeared into the barn.

Nights belonged to the midway. It was a garish world of spinning rides and come-on games, screaming teenagers and junk-food stands, hustlers and suckers. As a boy I had thought of the carnival as an exotic and illicit world. To sneak away to it, I fancied, would be like wandering through the harbor district of a tough city. Carnivals are tamer now, more like suburban amusement parks, but I cannot resist surrendering to their noise and light. A carnival is an exercise for the viscera, a taunting and tempting of innocence, a place to lose oneself in a crowd.

I drifted into a sideshow owned by Ward Hall and C. M. Christ of Gibsonton, Florida, one of the few such shows still operating in the country. A man with a ruffled blue shirt and cummerbund swallowed swords and threw knives toward a young woman. A dwarf named Poobah fondled a boa constrictor and picked up a 12-pound bucket by a hook stuck in his tongue. The young woman of the knife-throwing act, dressed in a tight, glittering-red body (Continued on page 187)

Truro, Iowa

Television meets a back roads celebrity as ABC's Sandy Hill interviews farmer Joe Hays. His invitation to Pope John Paul II brought the Pontiff to Iowa in 1979. "I felt the Pope would focus the world's attention on the concerns of rural America," said Hays. ABC interviewed him for "Good Morning America" a few weeks before the Pontiff's visit. At right, in the kitchen with his wife, Ann, and Sandy, Joe laughs about his encounter with a familiar barnyard hazard. At far right, Sandy rehearses her introductory remarks as the family gathers to shout, "Good morning America!"

Spencer, Iowa On a warm September evening, Ferris wheels turn high above the grounds of the Clay County Fair. In 1979, more than 280,000 attended the gathering, a

break from routine for both young and old. The fair's entertainments included games,
a sideshow, livestock competitions, and one of the country's largest exhibits of farm machinery.

*T*icket agent Leonard V. Farley, atop a
wooden platform, sizes up a growing
crowd gathering for a sneak preview of
the Clay County Fair's popular sideshow.
Painted banners on the tent behind him
promise unusual and amazing
attractions: a seven-foot giant, a daring
sword-swallower, a fire-eating dwarf.
"You've got to love all kinds of people to
endure the heat, dust, and other
headaches in this business," says Farley,
who has spent thirty years with traveling
sideshows. Other visitors find pleasure in
an evening stroll along avenues lined
with more than sixty amusement and food
stands (opposite, upper). Games of skill
and chance tempt all comers; ornately
costumed dolls reward winners at one
concessionaire's game (above).

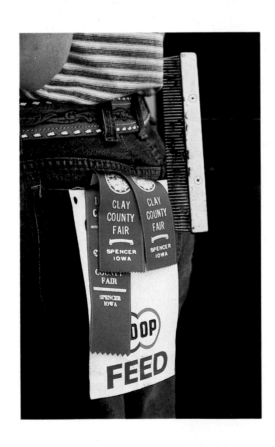

Farm machinery displays draw some fairgoers, and others compete for ribbons. The self-propelled combine (left) harvests 12 rows of corn at a time—and costs more than a hundred thousand dollars. Below, a young exhibitor urges his balky steer toward the wash rack, first step in readying the animal for showing. More than 900 people took part in livestock competitions and some 600 more in homemaking contests at the 1979 fair. Ribbons tucked in a back pocket (opposite, below) attest to skills in cattle raising. A grooming comb, alongside, comes in handy for touch-ups before the judging.

THOMAS O'NEILL, NATIONAL GEOGRAPHIC STAFF

suit and black net stockings, sat on an electrified chair and had torches lit from her tongue. The crowd watched, speechless.

The autumn nights were warm, and by eight o'clock the avenues of the midway were busy with people, most of them of high school age. "We appeal to teenagers. They can't be looking at cattle all the time," said Bernard Thomas, owner of the Mighty Thomas Shows, Inc., the company that has furnished carnival rides for the Clay County Fair for the last 24 years. Thomas remembers the days, as recently as 15 years ago, when freak shows and girlie revues were main carnival attractions. These elements have largely disappeared. "The carnival has gone full circle," Thomas observed. "It's now one of the few places a family can go and not see anything X-rated. For the customer to enjoy himself now, he has to get involved; he can't be a spectator. He has to throw a ball, or buy a ticket and take a ride."

I heeded the cries of the hawkers—rather polite at this fair—and did my share of participating. I threw balls at baskets, hoops, and milk cans. I tossed rings onto pop bottles and shot water into a clown's mouth. By night's end, I had prizes under my arms: a red pig, a tiger, a Snoopy doll with a broken neck. I rode the double Ferris wheel and the Yo-Yo and the Tilt-a-Whirl. I jumped a bit in the Screamhouse when a hag leaped up in my face and screeched. I laughed in the Astroliner, which is supposed to create the illusion that you have crashed into a canyon wall. Sometimes I joined the promenade of people, and we circled and circled, as if on a ride of our own.

Every step I took I was entreated by a carnival worker, or "carny." Do this, try that, don't be a chump, win a prize. Gradually I began to seek out their company. Some taught me the carnies' pig Latin. (Add "eaz" after the first syllable of a word.) They had slang for many things. An "alibi" once referred to a rigged game but now means simply a difficult one, like tossing a ring over the neck of a bottle. A "hanky pank" is an easy game, like knocking down bottles with a baseball. The harder the game, the larger the prizes. "Forty-second and Broadway" means a good location. Customers are simply "marks."

Shortly after midnight on one of the last days of the fair, the carnies held their end-of-the-season jamboree. About 75 of them gathered inside a bingo tent—gypsies, Indians, college graduates, dropouts, hangers-on. On the street in the light of day they would look like trouble. Inside the tent that night, they were special.

The jamboree is a once-a-year auction to raise money for showman's clubs, carny organizations that provide scholarships, burials, and emergency services for the carnival workers.

The evening was a rare one. Here was a host of itinerants united by altruism. It was a spectator sport just to watch them. As a storm threatened outside the tent, the carnies threw away prodigious amounts of money on raffle tickets and bingo cards. A fifth of Chivas Regal scotch was auctioned for fifty dollars; a water pipe went for

"Carnies"—carnival workers—celebrate in the bingo tent at season's end. Toni Del Rio (upper) hawks raffle tickets. Author Tom O'Neill (far left) and photographer Ira Block join in the festivities. Tom tries his hand at bingo; a triumphant Ira shows off his trophy—a teddy bear awarded by Jackie Townsend, a concessionaire. Proceeds from the annual party go to charity.

Northern Illinois *Sunset burnishes dust clouds wafting above cornfields of the Joe Faivre farm near De Kalb. Twin combines reap the October harvest from the 4,320-acre farm,*

one of the state's largest. It yielded 651,400 bushels in 1979, a record for the farm. Five of the seven Faivre children and a son-in-law share the work load of this family operation.

*C*autiously hanging on,
J. R. Faivre climbs the roof of
a 130-foot-high steel storage bin
that can hold 260,000 bushels of
corn. Nearby, Joe Faivre (above)
unloads a dump truck into an
underground hopper. The field
crew at right takes an afternoon
coffee break, a welcome rest in a
16-hour day that begins before
dawn. The long days continue for
eight weeks during the harvest.

twenty. The tables were thick with people drinking and talking and gambling—spending money just like the marks.

The party grew more and more boisterous. A man and a woman announced loudly that they were going to be married on the merry-go-round in two days. Two men began to scuffle; other carnies broke them up. A pig was roasting in a nearby tent. A can of insect repellent fetched five dollars.

At two o'clock in the morning rain began to fall heavily, and people started dashing to the food tent. Men and women began pairing off. Ira and I didn't know how to say goodbye, so we sprinted into the darkness and the storm, leaving the carnies to their night of celebration.

From Iowa, I looped into Wisconsin, where the hillsides were fiery with autumn leaves, and continued into Illinois, where the harvest season had begun. One day in early October, I stopped at the farm of Joseph Faivre, outside De Kalb. His is one of the largest farms in Illinois with its 4,320 cultivated acres—all corn—and one of the most up-to-date in terms of equipment. Despite the large size of the operation, Joe proudly calls it a family farm. Two sons and a son-in-law have formed a partnership with him, and another son is prepared to join in a few years, when he finishes school at the University of Illinois.

Harvest, of course, is the climax of a farmer's year, the "big deal," according to Joe's bearded 33-year-old son, J.R. The fussing with seed varieties, fertilizers, and weed control, the worried looks at the sky and the intense analysis of the grain market, the trust a farmer has—all lead up to this time when the harvesters learn what the land has to offer. Expectations and forebodings toss in the mind months before the first kernel is shelled. "At the beginning of July, you start to get psyched up for the harvest," J.R. explained. "By mid-August, you have the jitters. If you've ever been in a school play and remember how you felt the day before the first performance, you know the jitters. I have nightmares about neighboring farmers having all their work done before I even get started, or about not having enough men for the job."

I arrived at the Faivre farm at the end of the first week of harvest, by which time the jitters had been forgotten and the Faivres were preoccupied with making everything run smoothly. The harvest had not yet taken on its steady, obsessive rhythm. The work was coming in spurts because of a disrupting streak of wet weather and occasional breakdowns of equipment. By eight o'clock on my first morning, the farm's three combines had lumbered out to the fields. The Faivres headquartered themselves in the granary, where trucks unloaded the harvested corn. Inside a small cluttered room was an electronic control board, conceived and wired by Steve Faivre, 28, an engineering wizard. It indicated whether the dryers were running and how full they and the storage bins were. On a table stood a digital readout from the scale, which recorded the weight of each truckload of corn.

Every twenty minutes or so, a dump truck full of corn pulled into the granary and was weighed. It then spilled its yellow cargo through a grate in the floor into a hopper. From there the corn was transported by conveyor belts into a dryer, which thickened the air with a blizzard of chaff and reduced the moisture content of the corn so it could be stored. The dry corn then went by belt to mammoth storage bins capable of holding a total of 700,000 bushels. Last year, a record one for the farm, the Faivres nearly filled them. Most of the corn is eventually barged down the Mississippi River to New Orleans.

In the early afternoon, the harvest sputtered. It had started to rain, and the combines were called in. A conveyor belt had also malfunctioned. The Faivres and their crew spent the rest of the day in the shop, tinkering with machinery.

At one o'clock the next afternoon, the combines sallied forth again. I hitched a ride this time, accompanying 22-year-old Terry Hickey, foreman of the field crew. Slowly—at about three miles an hour—the combine waded into an expanse of eight-foot-high corn, taking six rows at a time. The stalks fell abruptly before the machine, dropping like dancers in a violently choreographed routine. Swath by swath, the combines leveled the fields. The combine's head—a clawlike metal extension—knocked the stalks down, stripped off the ears, and sent them rushing into the interior of the machine, where the kernels were rubbed off by a spinning cylinder. When the 175-bushel bin on the machine was full, an auger sprayed the kernels into a truck, which then headed back to the granary.

Terry denied being bored as he rides up and down identical fields. Sitting in his air-conditioned cab, he passes the time by figuring out where the combines should unload, listening to the radio, or practicing the spiel he uses in his weekend auctioning business. "My wife gets sick of hearing it at home," he said, "because I'm always selling her or the house." Harvesting consumes his life for the two months he drives in the fields. "My wife says I talk in my sleep about combining," he told me. "One night she said I sat straight up in bed. I must have thought I was combining. I asked her if she had brought the parts for my machinery."

Before I left the Faivres, I talked with Joe in the barn about prices and weather and equipment and family. After a while, he pulled off his cap and smiled. "It's always a good time to be a farmer," he concluded with a chuckle. "I have to be that optimistic."

The next few days passed in a blur. By now, autumn had ripened all around me. On the roadside were cider stands, and in the gardens rows of pumpkins. Daybreak was chilly, and small towns smelled of burning leaves. On Friday nights, marching bands could be heard playing at the high school football games. The fields of corn and soybeans were coming down, ready for the dormancy of winter. Yet I hardly noticed these things. I was making a dash for home.

I remembered from my reading of John Steinbeck's *Travels With Charley*—a man-and-dog-see-America book—that on the last days of his trip Steinbeck had quit talking with people, had stopped ruminating about his experiences. From the South, he drove feverishly to his home in New York City, neglecting even the scenery.

I sympathized with that homing instinct. Forging through Indiana and racing along the Ohio River, I had entered the same time zone as that of Washington, D.C., and was essentially only a mountain range away. For a while, all my thoughts turned to my arrival home. All the country I had seen, all the people I had talked with, and all the events I had witnessed were pushing me along, taking me back to the place where I had started.

On the last day of the trip my head cleared. How do I end this trip, this book? I wondered. I puzzled over this as I crossed into the West Virginia mountains, and before long I was lost. Of course. To be a traveler on the back roads, I reminded myself, requires a willingness to lose your way, to drive with no destination in mind. You have as much

West Virginia   *Roller-coaster country road pierces the scented woods of the Monongahela National Forest. "There's something about driving back roads," reflects Tom. "You never know what's around the next bend." As winter approaches, Tom and Ira head for home.*

time as the sun in the sky. And anyway, all roads end up somewhere.

When I realized I was lost, I was on a road barely wider than a driveway. The last town I recalled was Clay. By the side of the road, a river or creek always seemed to be running. Trees closed around me like the billowing walls of a tent. Back in the woods, I saw isolated houses, with dogs patrolling the front steps. There were no highway numbers or mileage posts. I kept driving, going from pavement to gravel, climbing ridges and dropping into unnamed valleys.

I had been eager to interview one more person and thus suitably close the trip. That last person turned out to be me.

I had learned early in my trip that back roads travel is therapeutic in that it encourages reverie. Wells of consideration open up. You ponder a romance or a work assignment, or imagine the activities of friends. As the road stretches before you, you transport yourself into the future and wonder where and how you will fit.

During my interview, I asked myself what impressions I had gathered from nine months of traveling, away from the cities and superhighways. And I answered that I had become aware of people's strong pride in their surroundings, as in the case of an Iowa farmer's inviting the Pope to his home state, or in the boosterism that had people from South Carolina or New Mexico or Wisconsin imploring me to believe that their slice of country was the finest. I discovered how community rituals, such as a Vermont town meeting or a midwestern county fair, retain a vitality and a purpose.

I answered that I had learned how an abiding sense of routine, as with a dairy farmer in the Berkshires or a fire lookout in California, lent continuity and stability to people's lives. In certain small towns, I had noticed how time hovered motionless, like a gull on an updraft; in other places, change had permeated the fabric of life, as in a town in Alabama where a black man had been elected mayor, or on the plains of south Texas where a cattle rancher ruefully had admitted that he should spend more of his time at his desk than on his horse.

People I met often groused about national and international affairs. Yet I also saw how these people held an optimistic faith in the future, as with an Illinois corn farmer trusting that this year's crop would be a bumper one, or a Texas oil driller believing year after year that he would one day have wells of his own. Finally, I found that as a cross-country traveler I had become a leading character in a marvelous, continually unfolding drama. There was no end to the scenes that had stimulated and enlightened me.

I spent my last night on the road in Elkins. However much I had begun to visualize home, somehow this October night in West Virginia did not seem like the end. No, the trip would continue. In my mind, I would again check into a hotel next to the railroad tracks, and the train would be passing by, and the whistle would take hold and pull me into the distance, the only marker I require. Yes, ahead is the horizon, a town, a river, a mountain, a farm. Ahead is a road.

Index

Boldface indicates illustrations;
italic refers to picture legends

Aguero, Ralph 126-127, *131,* 133
Airplanes 141, *143,* **146, 147,** 151; crop dusting **132**
Alabama 9, 76-77, **81-83**
Alaska 9, *96,* 139-151; map **96**
Albany, Texas *106,* 107, 112, 116
Alicata, Jim 17
Allen, Jack **95**
Amish **4-5, 50-51**
Animas Peak, N. Mex. **116-117**
Apache 118, 125 *see also* White Mountain Apache
Arcadia Plantation, S. C. 69-70, 71, **72-73**
Archaeologists *96,* 119, 122-126
Arizona *96,* 107, 119-126
Ashby Gap, Va. **56-57**
Auctions **66-67,** *159,* 177, 187, 193
Augusta, Mont. **158-159,** *162*
Ayden, N. C.: barbecue 64-65

Baer, Robbie 125-126
Baker, Robert 93, **94**
Banda, Betty *endpapers*
Barbecues: North Carolina *55,* 63-65
Barbershop: Vermont 22, 23, **26-27**
Beaudoin, Pamphile "Barb" *endpapers,* 23, **27,** 33
Belgrade, Mont. 155, **156-157**
Beltrán, James **131**
Berendes, Charity *157*
Berkshire Hills, Mass.: dairy farm **14-15,** 16-17, 20-21, 194
Bible belt: Georgia 75-76
Biggs, Robert *endpapers*
Biggs, "Skeet" **167**

Bingo **186,** 187
Bisnett, Bud **159**
Black Hills, S. Dak. 164, 170-171, **172-174**
Black Range, N. Mex. **108-109,** 118; museum 117
Blacks 69, 71, **74, 94;** blues musicians *55,* 89-91, **92;** mayor 76-77, **81;** nonviolent protest march 76; slaves 69, 71, *73, 75;* voter registration 76
Blairsville Christian Center, Ga. 75-76, **78-79**
Bledsoe, Sybil Andersen *endpapers*
Bluegrass festival: Talkeetna, Alaska 141, **144-145**
Blues musicians *55,* 89-91, **92**
Boomtowns 107, *109,* 117
Brasstown Bald, Ga. 75
Brewster, Thomas **158**
Brookgreen Gardens, S. C. 70-71, **73**
Brookgreen Plantation, S. C. 69
Buford, Sarah 80, **87,** 88
Burgwyn, W. H. S., Jr. 65, **70**
Bush pilots: Alaska *96,* 141, **146,** 151
Butler, Ritchey 93, **95**
Byrd, Brian 125

Cadwallader, Len 22
Calhoun, John C. 65
California 9, *96,* 119, 126-135, 138-139, 151
Canyon Creek, Ariz. **122-123**
"carnies" (carnival workers) *152,* 177, **182-183, 186,** 187, 192
Carroll, Debbie **94**
Castro, Laura Garcia **131**
Cattle: branding 105; Charolais

51; county fair 176, beef auction 177, competitions 176, *181,* **184-185,** *185;* ear tagging **101,** 105; estates 153; Holstein 17, 52; Jersey **14-15,** 16-17, 20; milk cow, price of 17, 58; Texas longhorn 8, 97-101, 104-105; veterinarian **45,** 51-53
Cattlemen 97-105, 107
Cavaliers (bachelor society) 89
Cheronis, Kristin *endpapers,* **124,** 125
Children: art 155, **156-157,** 160; county fair 176-177; ranch work 97, **100-101,** 104-105; rural health care 161, *168,* **168;** town meeting 32
Chloride, N. Mex. **108-111**
Chodistaas, Ariz.: pueblo **122**
Christenberry, John *endpapers,* **82, 83**
Chugach Mountains, Alaska **142**
Cich, Joe **137**
Civil War 65, *70*
Clay County Fair, Iowa 176-177, **180-186,** 187, 192
Clute, Myron **42,** 44, 50
Cole, Mrs. James Pierce, Jr. 80
Cole, Katherine Ann *endpapers*
Collinsville, Vt. 22, 31-32, 33
Combines 177, **184-185, 188,** 192, 193
Connecticut 11, *12,* 14-16
Conservation: animal sanctuaries 70; lobster season *37,* 41, 43; *see also* Waterfowl
Copa de Vino (ranch), Texas **100-101,** 104, 105; roundup 97-102, 104-105
Corn *191,* **191,** 192, 193; fields 17, 171, 176, **188-189,** 192-193; *see also* Combines
County fair *see* Clay County Fair, Iowa
Cowhands 97, **101, 102-103,** 104, 105
Craftsbury, Vt. 22, *25,* **26-29,** 32-33
Craftsbury Common, Vt. 22, 23, **24-25,** 32, 33
Crazy Horse (monument), S. Dak. 164, l70-171, *172, 174;* scale model **172**
Crown Point Road, Vt. 21
Cruse, Mrs. A. C. **1**
Culbertson, Nancy **134, 135**
Custer, George Armstrong 161

Dairy farms: Massachusetts **14-**

Acknowledgments

The Special Publications Division is grateful to the individuals and organizations portrayed, named, or quoted in the text and to those listed here for their generous cooperation and assistance during the preparation of this book: David Ahl, John R. Alden, John Anderson, Don Avery, Sabina Barach, Robert C. Bayer, Polly M. Brown, Bill Cadola, Theodore R. Dudley, Alfredo D. Duran, Frank Durazo, L. Tuffly Ellis, Gary A. Fouts, Bob Gerhard, Sid Groff, Al Grouleff, Lanier Harper, Harold Haswell, David L. Hessman, John N. Hoffman, Michael Hughes, Charles Joyner, Clyde Lammott, Douglas D. Martin, Donna McMillan, Diana Murphy, Storrs L. Olson, Jay Orr, Lyle Paul, Alan Perlis, Joe Posewitz, Charles A. Ratté, George C. Rogers, Jr., Dan Scheffey, Walter G. Seibert, Stanwyn G. Shetler, Tom Waite, Flora Weeks, Mrs. Lyman Wilkins, Mr. and Mrs. Lyman Wilkins, Jr.; *Low Rider* magazine, the Center for Southern Folklore.

15, 16-17, 20, 194; Pennsylvania **45,** 51-53
Dale, Pi **86**
Debutantes *see* Southern Debutante Assembly
Deckard, Brenda **94**
DeClay, Janet *endpapers,* **121**
DeClay, Ronette **121**
De Kalb, Ill.: farm near **188-191,** 192-193
Deerfield River, Vt. **30**
Del Rio, Toni **186**
Delaplane, Va. *56, 63,* 65
Des Moines, Iowa: Pope John Paul II's Mass 175, 176
Dohnalek, Mary 125-126
Douglass, Texas 91, 93, **94-95**
Dunkin, Benjamin 69
Dunkin, Benjamin Faneuil 65, 69
Durham, Conn. 15-16
Dutch Gulch, N. Mex.: gold claim **114-117,** 118-119
Dyer, Danny 76

East Craftsbury, Vt. 22, 23, 31
Eddy Gulch lookout, Calif. **134-135**
Eden Mountain Boys **26**
Edison, Robert **101**
Emerson, Isaac 69-70
Entertainment and recreation: cribbage *41;* eight-ball pool 23, 33; mail-boat arrival 41; matching quarters 41; outdoor **4-5, 50-51,** television **116;** *see also* Clay County Fair; "lowriders"; Music
Evans, Semmes 89

Faivre, Joseph **191,** 192, 193; family *189,* **190,** 192-193; farm **188-191**
Family traditions *63;* barbecue business 64; inheritance 17, 52, 69-70, *70, 127, 163*
Farley, Leonard V. **182**
Farm and Wilderness Foundation *18,* **18-19,** 21-22
Farm machinery 17, 177 *see also* Combines
Farms; farmland **5,** *50,* 52, **56-57,** 58, 69, **132,** *148, 152,* 153, 155, 171, 176, **188-191,** 192-193 *see also* Dairy farms; Horse farms
Farrar, Bill **29,** 33
Ferris, William 90-91
Fielders, Perley **28,** 33
Fish houses: Maine **38, 40,** 41

Fishing, sport 59, 62-63, **68**
Fishing boats **36-39,** 41, 43; skiffs **39,** 62-63, **68**
Fletcher, Earl *endpapers,* **14,** 16-17, 20; family 16-17, 20
Flynn, Michael 54, 58
Foraker, Mount, Alaska 141
Forests 21, 43, 70, 75, 76, *137,* **154, 195;** fires *96,* 133, 138, 139, lookouts *96, 111,* 133, **134-135,** 138-139; products **34-35,** 43-44, **136-137,** 139
Fort Apache Indian Reservation, Ariz. 119, **120-121**
Fort Kent, Maine **35,** 44
Frederickson, Charles "Al" 133, 138-139

Gainesville, Va.: horse farm near 54, 58, *59*
Game warden *152,* 153, **158, 159**
Garza, Hill **103**
General stores 22-23, **63,** 65, 76, **112-113,** 118; variety 41
Georgetown, S. C.: rice plantations near 65, 69-70, 74-75
Georgia **1,** *55,* 75-76, **78-79**
Ghost towns **108-109,** *109,* **110-111**
Glanville, Hal **169**
Gold mining: Alaska *150;* California 119; New Mexico *96, 113,* **114-115,** 118-119
Goldendale, Wash. *140;* observatory **138,** 139
Goliad, Texas 97, **104;** ranch near *see* Copa de Vino
Goodwin, Neil 33
Graduation, high school *55,* 91, 93, **94-95**
Grasshopper, Ariz.: pueblo 125
Green Mountain Boys 21
Green Mountains, Vt. 16; ice harvesting **18-19,** 21-22; summer camps *18,* 21, 22
Greenwood, Miss.: debutante ball 80; plantation near *see* Nebo Plantation
Griggs, Eleanor 31
Griggs, Lawrence 31

Hale County, Ala. **82-83**
Hall, Steve 139
Harbin, Patti 88-89
Harris, Patricia **74**
Hayden, Andrew M. 76-77, **81**
Hays, Ann *endpapers,* 175, **178**

Hays, Joe *endpapers,* 171, 175-176, **178;** children 175, **179**
Hayter, Phyllis **94**
Henry Standing Bear (Sioux chief) 164, 170
Herbs, medicinal **42,** 44, 50
Hickey, Terry 193
High schools 32 *see also* Graduation
Hill, Sandy 175, 176, **178, 179**
Hillsboro, N. Mex. **112-113,** *115,* 117-119
Hitchhikers **144**
Holdcroft, Roy **101, 103**
Homer, Alaska 140, *148*
Homesteading: Alaska *148, 150*
Horse farms: Virginia 54, 58-61
Horses 21, **72,** 97, 105, 160, 161; Morgan horses 11, **13,** 14-15, 16; quarterhorses **100-101;** *see also* Thoroughbreds
Hudson, Cliff *endpapers,* 141, **146,** 151; family 141, 151
Hoppe, Henry R. 15-16
Hughesville, Md. *66*
Hunting 62; preserve 69; season *159*
Huntington, Anna Hyatt 70
Huntington, Archer M. 70, 71

Ice cutting: industry 21
Ice harvesting: Vermont pond *8, 10,* **18-19,** 21-22

Library of Congress CIP Data

O'Neill, Thomas, 1951-
 Back roads America.

 Includes index.
 1. United States—Social life and customs—1971- 2. United States—Description and travel—1960- 3. O'Neill, Thomas, 1951- I. Block, Ira. II. National Geographic Society, Washington, D. C. Special Publications Division.
E169.02.O55 973 78-21448
ISBN 0-87044-282-1, regular binding
ISBN 0-87044-287-2, library binding

Composition for *Back Roads America* by Composition Systems Inc., Arlington, Va. Printed and bound by Holladay-Tyler Printing Corp., Rockville, Md. Color separations by The Beck Engraving Co., Philadelphia, Pa.; The Lanman Companies, Washington, D. C.; National Bickford Graphics, Inc., Providence, R.I.; Progressive Color Corp., Rockville, Md.; and The J. Wm. Reed Co., Alexandria, Va.

Idaho **154**
Illinois **188-191,** 192-193, 194
Indians of North America *see*
    Apache; Mogollon; Mohawk;
    Sioux
Iowa **9,** 171, 175, 176-187, 194

Jácome, Phil 125-126
James, Elmore 90
Jenkins, Herbert, Jr. *endpapers,*
    62-63, **68**
Jenkins, Mary **74**
Jersey Acres Farm, Mass. **14-15,**
    16-17, 20
John Paul II, Pope 171, 175,
    176, *178,* 194
Johnson, Jerry *endpapers,* **102,**
    103
Johnson, Michael 125-126
Johnson, Myles 176
Johnson, Robert 89
Johnston, J. T. (Doctor Tom)
    160-161, **165-169**
Jones, Walter "Pete" 64-65
"jook joints" 76, 90

Kahiltna Glacier, Alaska 151
Kamiah, Idaho *154*
Keck, George **45,** 51-53
Kelley, Wofford *endpapers,* **78**
Kenai Mountains, Alaska **143**
Key, Lydia 117
Kilcher, Yule **148, 149**
King, Carolyn Joyce *endpapers*
King, Martin Luther, Jr. 76
Klamath National Forest, Calif.
    133, **134-135,** 138-139
Kohn, Sandy *endpapers*
Korczak ("Storyteller in Stone")
    see Ziolkowski, Korczak

Lachicotte, A. H. "Doc" 69, 71,
    74, 75
Lachicotte, Philip Rossignol 69
La France, Martha 44
Lagacé, Joe *endpapers,* **35**
Lake Mountain, Calif.: lookout
    133, 138-139
Leas, Louie Strother ("Teenie")
    endpapers, 65
Lebanon Valley, Pa.: dairy
    farms **45,** 51-52
Leland, Miss. 89, *93*
Licking, George, Jr. **168**
Linhart, "Judge" **102**
Lobstering *10;* boats **36-39,** 43;
    equipment **38, 39, 40,** 41, 43;
    "keepers" *38,* size *43;* season
    37, 41, 43
Long, Thomas R. 76

Lost Mountain, Va. **56-57**
Low Country, S. C. 65, 69, **72-75,**
    75
"lowriders" *96,* 126-127, **128-**
    131, 133

McCants, Jim 118, 119
McCravey, Dave *endpapers,* **114,**
    116, 118, 119
McGrady, Phyllis 175
McKinley, Mount, Alaska 141,
    144, 147, 151
McMillan, Mrs. John Thomas
    80
Maine *10,* 11, 33-41, 43-44
Mangas, Jessica **157**
Maps **6-7,** *10, 55, 96,* **152-153**
Marsh, John D. 54, 58
Marsh Thoroughbred Farm,
    Va. 54, 58-61
Maryland: tobacco auction **66-**
    67
Masonheimer, Ed 138, 139
Maskell, Allan 31
Massachusetts **14-15,** 16-17, 20,
    31, 141
Matanuska, M. V. (ferry) 139-
    140
Mathews, Carroll 11, **13,** 14-15,
    16; family 11, 14-16
Medical clinics, rural: Wyoming
    160-161, *165,* **167-169**
Medicine men, Mohawk *10,* **42,**
    44, 50
Mendota, Calif. 126-131, 133
Mennonites *50*
Mexican Americans 126;
    "lowriders" *96,* 126-127, **128-**
    131, 133
Middle Creek Wildlife Manage-
    ment Area, Pa. **4-5, 46-51,** 53
Middlebury, Conn. 11, 14-15
Midway Plantation, S. C. 65, 69,
    71
Mihalovich, Paul 153, **158, 159**
Milstead, James H. 93
Milstead, Steven **94**
Mississippi *55,* 80, **84-88,** 88-89,
    90, 91, **92;** delta 77, 80, 90
Mobile homes **116,** 118, 119
Mogollon 119, *122,* 125
Mohawk *10,* **42,** 44, 50-51
Monhegan Island, Maine *10,* **36-**
    40, 41, 43
Monongahela National Forest,
    W. Va. **195**
Montana 152-153, 155-160, **162-**
    163
Montjoy, Mrs. William Hem-
    ingway 80

Mount Arena Plantation, Sandy
    Island, S. C. 71
Mount Rushmore National
    Memorial, S. Dak. 164
Mountain climbers: Alaska 141,
    144, 147, 151
Music; musicians: bluegrass
    141, **144-145;** blues *55,* 89-91,
    92; country *26,* 31-32,
    fiddlers 31, 33; flute **148;**
    garden party 89; guitarists 31,
    89-91, **92, 94**

Naranjo, Paula **131**
National Register of Historic
    Places: Prospect Hill, S. C. 70
Nebo Plantation, near Schlater,
    Miss. 80, **84-88,** 88-89
Neckstad, Odin **159**
New Mexico *96,* 107, 108-119,
    194
New York *42,* 44, 50-51
North Carolina *55,* 58, 63-65,
    68, *70*
Northwind (fishing boat) **39,** 43
Northeast (region) 11-53; map
    10

O'Brack, Pat *endpapers,* **117**
Oil *168;* backyard wells **106,** 107,
    112, 116; stripper wells 112,
    113
Oregon **136-137,** *137,* 139
Outlaws: New Mexico 118

Packer's Corner Farm, Vt.:
    letterboxes **20**
Pate, Elizabeth **124**
Pate, Lucille 69-70, *73,* **73**
Pate, Wallace 69, **73**
Pelletier, Harold **34**
Pennsylvania **4-5, 45,** 46-53
Perkins, Vickie 93, **95**
Pinedale, Wyo. *166;* medical
    clinic 160-161, **168-169**
Pit houses 119, 125
Plant introduction: kudzu *90*
Plant medicines: herbs **42,** 44, 50
Plant study center 70
Plantations *see* Arcadia; Brook-
    green; Midway; Mount
    Arena; Nebo; True Blue;
    Waverly
Plymouth, Vt. *see* Farm and
    Wilderness Foundation
Powell, Pattie **61**
Prospect Hill (estate), S. C. 70
Pueblos, Mogollon **122,** 125-126

Quebec Province, Canada:

Indian reservation 44
Quilts, handmade 75

Raboin's Village Store,
Craftsbury, Vt. 22-23
Radio shows: Midwest 171
Ranchers 8, 119 *see also*
Cattlemen
Ranches; rangeland 97-102,
104-105, 160, 161, **162,** *165,*
168
Rayfield, Buzz 127
Rawls, Henry **68**
Reid, J. Jefferson *endpapers,* **123,**
125
Revival meetings: Georgia *55,*
75-76, **78-79**
Rice-plantation sites: South
Carolina *55,* 65, 69-71, 74-75
Roadside stands: cider 193;
produce **1;** quilts 75
Rocky Mountains 152, 155, **162-**
163
Runge, Texas: bar **102-103;**
ranch near *see* Copa de Vino
Rushmore, Mount, S. Dak.:
carving of 164, 170

St. John, Maine **34-35**
St. Regis Indian Reservation,
N. Y.–Quebec *42,* 44; size 44
Salisbury, Judy *endpapers,* 155
San Joaquin Valley, Calif. 126,
131, 133, *133*
Sandy Island, S. C. 71, **75**
Schlater, Miss.: plantation near
see Nebo
Schmidt, Raymond *endpapers,*
110
Schmitt, Michael 32, 33
Schmitt, Penny 32
Schoolhouses: one-room 155,
156; two-room **27**
Scott, Walter 97, *99,* **99, 100,**
103, 104-105, 107; family 97,
100, 101, 104-105
Sculptures: environmental art
155, **156-157,** 160; garden 70-
71; mountain 164, 170-171,
172, scale model **172**
Sell, Raymonde **165**
Selma, Ala. 76
Shoshone, Calif.: sign **127**
Silver-mining town: New Mexico
108-111
Simpson, Jean *endpapers,* 23, 31,
33; father 23
Sioux 161, 164, 170
Sitka, Alaska 140
Sleigh rides 11, **13,** 14-15, 16;

rally *13,* 15-16
Slicer, Robert 23
Small, Susan "Pigeon" *end-*
papers, **74**
Sorrells, Bernice *endpapers,* **127**
South (region) 54-95; map **55**
South Carolina *55,* 65, 69-75,
194
South Dakota 164, 170-174
Southern Debutante Assembly:
doyennes 80; garden party
55, 80, **84-88,** 88-89
Southwest (region) 107-126, 194
Spaniards, early *99*
Spencer, Iowa: county fair 176-
177, **180-186,** 187, 192
Springhill School, Mont.: art
program 155, **156-157,** 160
Stanley, Sherman **40,** 43
Stanley, Sherman, Jr. **38, 39, 40,**
41, 43; family *endpapers,* 43
Strouphar, Charlie 53
Sunrise Dance **120-121**
Swan, Dale **167**

Talkeetna, Alaska 140, 141, **144-**
145, *150*
Tallichet, Judie *endpapers,* 155,
156, 160
"Tanana Grass" **144**
Tarbox, Gurdon, Jr. 70, 71
Tarrant, Joey **95**
Television: "Good Morning
America" 175-176, **178-179**
Texas 8, *55, 87,* 90, 91, 93, **94-**
95, *96,* 97-107, 112-113, 116
Thomas, Allie 75
Thomas, Bernard 187
Thomas, James "Son" *endpapers,*
89-91, **92**
Thomas, Raymond 91
Thoroughbreds 54, *55,* 58-61
Thunderhead Mountain, S.
Dak. 164, 170-171, **172-174**
Tidmore, Morris *endpapers,* **106,**
107, 112-113, 116
Tobacco auction **66-67**
Tobacco-burning ritual 44, 50
Town meetings: Vermont 22,
28-29, 32-33, 194
Townsend, Jackie **186**
Tree-clearing: Alaska **148-149**
True Blue Plantation, S. C. 69,
71
Truro, Iowa: farm near 175-
176, **178-179**
Tuggle, H. David **122**
Turnagain Arm, Alaska **142-143**

Uniontown, Ala. 76-77, **81**

United States: map-painting **6-7**
U. S. Forest Service 133, 138-139
U. S. Route 1 44; marker **35**
University of Arizona: archae-
ological field school 119, **122-**
124, 125

Valdez, Alex 127
Vanderbilt, Cornelius 69
Vanderbilt, George 69
Vaughan, Louise **86**
Vermont 8, *10,* **12-13,** 16, **18-20,**
21-33
Veterinarian **45,** 51-53
Virginia 54-61, **63,** 65
Voting: Alabama 76, 77, *81,*
registering of blacks 76;
Vermont 22, **29,** 33

Waccamaw River, S. C. *75;* rice
plantations 65, 69-71
Wagner, Jenny *endpapers,* **157**
Washington, Rebecca ("Miss
Becca") 71
Washington (state) *138,* 139,
140
Waterfowl: migration *5, 47,* 53;
preserve **4-5, 46-49,** 53
Waverly Plantation, S. C. 69
Webb, Ken and Susan *end-*
papers, 22
Weber, Peggy **169**
Wells, George 118-119
Wells, Mildred **29**
West Virginia 193-194, **195**
Whitaker, Jim **94**
White Mountain Apache 119,
120-121
Whitney, Leslie **39,** 43
Wildlife 31, 33, *63,* 69, 70, 71,
74, 139, 153, 155 *see also*
Waterfowl
Williamson, Sonny Boy 89
Wilson, Earl 32
Winter wheat: field **140**
Women: farmhands 16, 54, 58,
61, 105; lobstering **39,** 43
Woodland, N. C. 65, *70*
Wyoming **2-3,** *152,* 160-161,
165-169, 170

Youth: Amish **4-5, 50-51;** county
fair 176, 177, **185,** 187;
summer camp 21, 22; ranch
work 97, **100-101,** 104-105;
see also High schools

Ziolkowski, Korczak *endpapers,*
164, 170-171, **173;** family
164, 170, **174**

JOE LAGACÉ
ST. JOHN, MAINE

ANN AND JOE HAYS
TRURO, IOWA

KORCZAK ZIOLKOWSKI
BLACK HILLS, SOUTH DAKOTA

JUDY SALISBURY
SPRINGHILL SCHOOL
BELGRADE, MONTANA

SANDY KOHN
SALT ASH MOUNTAIN,
VERMONT

MORRIS TIDMORE
ALBANY, TEXAS

SUSAN AND KEN WEBB
PLYMOUTH, VERMONT

BETTY BANDA
MENDOTA, CALIFORNIA